BEYOND THE OPEN ·CLASSROOM: TOWARD INFORMAL EDUCATION

By Lorraine L. Morgan, Vivien C. Richman and Ann Baldwin Taylor

C²¹

CENTURY TWENTY ONE PUBLISHING

PUBLISHED BY

CENTURY TWENTY ONE PUBLISHING
POST OFFICE BOX 8
SARATOGA, CALIFORNIA 95070

C **21**

LIBRARY OF CONGRESS CARD CATALOG NUMBER

80-69235

I.S.B.N.

0-86548-050-8

TABLE OF CONTENTS

INTRODUCTION

This book has been written in response to rising numbers of requests for help from teachers, principals, chief school administrators and parents on how to implement the informal approach to education. Many books and articles have been published, many conference papers have been delivered, each dealing with different aspects of informal education.

It is the intent of the writers to provide the pre-service or in-service educator, administrator or parent with a guidebook which is easy to read and which is written from a practical point of view. This book has grown out of our experiences in American and British classrooms, and pre-service and in-service workshops with teachers and administrators.

We have observed, in these experiences, that several issues and questions arise each time. It is those issues to which we will address ourselves in this manuscript.

One of our objectives, for example, is to assist the reader in understanding the philosophy and the assumptions upon which informal education is based and, without which, no meaningful beginning may be made.

A second objective is to examine sources of the impetus and impact of change in the schools which are being expressed by different ways of looking at children and learning. Emphasis is placed on finding ways to individualize, personalize and humanize learning in the classroom.

The book is designed to offer practical advice on how to move toward informal education through non-gradedness, team teaching and differentiated staffing. It explores grouping patterns and problems of organization and scheduling. Concrete suggestions are given in considering the arrangement of the learning environment, the development of learning centers, and the utilization of materials, equipment and the environment surrounding the school.

A recurring concern, which is examined, is the need for effective means of evaluation and assessment of the growth and development of individual children. Similarly, the process of communication between school and home is explored.

The book concludes with a discussion about the preparation of teachers, both preservice and inservice for informal education. The reader is left with some questions to consider in the light of his own values and commitments.

CHAPTER 1

INSIDE AN INFORMAL CLASSROOM

A Conventional Setting

The first day of school! What images come to mind...
children still shining with summer sun, awkward and self-conscious
in new school clothes, their feet reluctantly encased in stiff new
shoes, their faces eager, shy, uncertain, excited. The bell
strieks in the school yard and the lines of children form. The
summer is over.

Inside, in classrooms that are tidy and ordered, the
newly-decorated bulletin boards proclaim "Welcome Back To School!"
as each child finds himself a desk in a row of desks and is duly
recorded in the teacher's seating chart. The teacher introduces
himself and clearly establishes his authority. The children are
introduced to the "rules of the room," either as laid down by the
teacher, or as the product of a discussion. The children are
pretty much aware of what is expected of them in the "discussion"
and the lists of rules in various rooms tend to resemble each
other. "We will sit in our seats. We will be quiet. We will
listen. We will not fight. We will do our work. We will not
talk.." and so on. The bells ring, and at set intervals the children move into well-established, pre-set routines, and the whole
dreary, deadening process is begun. There is little time left
for laughter and joy...it's time to quit playing around and get
down to work.

An Informal Classroom

How different the first day of school could be! What follows is a composite, and, therefore, hypothetical description of
another kind of beginning. The scene is The New School, located
in the United States serving primary children from ages 5 to 8,

and featuring team teaching, non-gradedness, vertical age grouping and differentiated staffing. The school is organized on the philosophy of informal education.

8:00   The teachers are quietly excited, full of anticipation
        moving around swiftly, setting out materials and books
        for the children.

8:30   The children begin to come in, some smiling and happy,
        others timid, cautious. They walk around rather quietly,
        some beginning to get acquainted with each other, others
        looking at books and other materials. There are beautiful
        samples of children's work...poetry, paintings, and
        drawings on the bulletin boards.

9:00   The team leader or pod leader invites the children to
        assemble, by moving quietly among them with a gentle
        "Come along, children." There are no bells! They sit
        quietly on the floor and the teacher introduces himself
        and the staff, welcoming them all to school. He invites
        the children to explore the classroom freely, as they
        have been doing and to return in 15 minutes.

9:15   The children reassemble and are led into a game which
        helps them to learn each other's names. The teacher
        then identifies each child correctly by name. The chil-
        dren cannot conceal their delight and astonishment! Each
        child has been recognized individually. "He knows me...
        he knows me!" they cry out. A nice personalized touch.

        The teacher goes on to explain how they are going to
        learn how to live together harmoniously, with a few
        simple ground rules. "You are free to move about to
        work, but you may not interfere with anyone else's learn-
        ing. You may use whatever materials and equipment you
        need, but you may not destroy things..." He outlines
        the few simple rules concerning health and safety.

Most of the children are listening attentively, but a
few are fussing, interrupting and talking to each other.
The teacher's voice changes. His voice grows stern. Now,
all the children are listening. "A few of you," he says,
"have been acting silly and rude. We have to try to live
here together. We will really have to think of one
another. There are many beautiful things here and there
are many exciting things to do. Silly and rude behavior
will get in our way." It is very quiet as the message
is absorbed. The teacher's expectations are clear.

10:00   Each child is given a plastic tote box in which to keep
        his belongings. The teacher suggests that they put their
        names on it or paste a picture of themselves on it and
        store it in the rack. The children are invited to choose
        an activity - reading, coloring or drawing. They group
        themselves in twos and threes and go about their tasks
        quietly. The teachers move around, offering suggestions
        to the timid and answering questions.

10:30   Everyone assembles again, after putting materials away,
        for informal folk singing. They sing some familiar songs
        and introduce some new ones, talking informally about
        what they are saying and where they come from. The
        session has a lovely quality, marked by joyful voices
        and friendly dialogue.

10:45   Recess and a snack. Some of the children remain inside
        to continue reading or drawing. Most of them go out to
        play.

11:00   "Come along, children." The children organized into two
        groups, the fives and sixes in one group and the sevens
        and eights in the other. The younger children listen to
        some funny poems which they discuss and decide to illus-
        trate. The older children listen to the story of "The
        Red Balloon" and talk about it until, suddenly, it is

time for lunch and recess.

1:00   The children return and are invited to take a book from
       the library and look at it quietly. This has a remarkable
       calming effect and they settle down, some reading alone,
       some sharing a book, reading to each other, talking
       quietly. There are a few problems with restless boys.
       The teachers talk with individual children, beginning
       informal assessment of them.

2:00   They come together again for some informal singing. There
       are the beginnings of a feeling of "group" which has been
       nurtured by singing together.

2:30   Again, two groups are formed. The younger children are
       talking about names and birthdays and the teacher develops
       a chart with them. The older children are discussing
       where they were born, using a map to locate birthplaces.

2:15   Recess, then cleaning up time. Everything is put away
       in its proper place, ready to be used again.

3:15   The last meeting. The teachers review the day with the
       children and look ahead to tomorrow.

       Overall impressions: An excellent first day. The out-
       standing characteristics have been joyfulness and diver-
       sity of children. The teachers are working together
       easily and smoothly, making contact, easing fears, un-
       tangling knots. It will take a while to develop a sense
       of community. Some of the children will obviously need
       to be "de-educated" and then retaught in this approach.
       Staff spirits are high after such a beautiful day.

The School, The Child, The Teacher

       The school is characterized by the use of the "integrated
day". This means, in effect, that the school day is not arbi-

trarily divided into time segments, each earmarked for a different activity. Rather, the children and the adults are free to pursue their natural interests without artificial or arbitrary interruption.

As a social community, the children and adults come together, as needed, in informal meetings, to discuss common problems, to develop ground rules, and to seek solutions to the problems of growing and living together. The program is further characterized by the procedure of "vertical age grouping" which enables children of all ages to collaborate with each other on projects of mutual interest - to instruct, advise and stimulate each other.

The learning environment is rich, varied and inviting, offering an array of books at various levels, art materials, mathematics apparatus such as balances, scales and games, writing materials, plants, animals and other science materials, etc. The use of the arts, music, drama, dance, graphic art, and crafts, such as weaving, needle work, pottery, dyeing, print-making and cooking, occupy a central and continuous role in the activities of the school. They function as auxiliary languages through which the children are encouraged to share and report their activities, discoveries and feelings. They also serve to unify and integrate the various subject areas.

The curriculum grows out of the interactions of the children and the adults with the environment. It can be described as "organic" in that it is constantly growing and branching with the interests and curiosities of the children and adults.

The teachers are partners and colleagues in learning with children, rather than acting as adversaries and guardians of "the right answer". They actively join the children in the search for knowledge and understanding. The teacher, in this setting, is an acute observer, a guide, an advisor and a questioner. He offers, presents, introduces, suggests and grows with the children.

The child, in this setting, is an explorer and adventurer. He is free to be and to become himself because there is no preconceived sequence of activities through which he is compelled to pass. The program is designed to fit the child. He acquires academic skills as he becomes ready for them and as they become relevant to his activities and his needs. He is expected to become responsible for his own learning, with appropriate guidance, support and instruction readily available to him. There is no "failure" in the conventional sense. The child gains confidence in himself as a learner, a seeker and a problem-solver. He learns to value the intrinsic rewards of his own accomplishments.

Some Underlying Assumptions

1. Every child has a need to know, a need to learn, to understand, to master, to order his world.

2. Each child is unique. Although he shares certain human characteristics with other children, he brings to the school a unique personality, his own learning style, experiences, cultural heritage, deficits, gifts and perceptions.

3. There is creativity and potential for natural learning in each child which can be nurtured and developed.

4. Social-emotional development must accompany cognitive-academic growth. Opportunities for both must be available throughout the school day in an integrated fashion.

5. An environment of mutual trust and respect among children, parents, staff, etc., provides the optimal learning situation.

6. The learner is an active participant in the learning process rather than being viewed as an empty vessel to be filled.

7. The active application of the principles of democracy to school practices is the most effective means of producing intelligent citizens for a democratic, pluralistic society.

Furthermore, the most desirable learning situation is one in which:

> ...The child feels welcome, where he is valued and respected as a person, and where he learns to value and respect others,

> ...The child is liberated from the artificial time divisions in the school day, and is free to explore the objects of his natural wonder and curiosity,

> ...The child learns to be aware of and trust his feelings, to be able to share his creative expressions with others,

...The child is encouraged to create and respond to beauty in all its forms and expressions,

...The child and the teacher become partners and collaborators in the quest for understanding and knowledge,

...The child is helped to discover the inter-relatedness of content areas,

...The child acquires skills as he becomes ready for them and as the acquisition of these skills becomes relevant to his activities and interests,

...The child learns both independent study and work skills and the interpersonal skills necessary for group activities and cooperative projects,

...The child is continually self-motivated as a result of his successes and achievements,

...The child learns to value the intrinsic rewards of his own accomplishments,

...The child develops a growing confidence in his competencies as a learner,

...The child learns to view the adults in the school as resource people and guides to whom he may turn for assistance.

Growth toward an informal classroom and the integrated day is gradual and painstaking. Problems and options for solution will be presented in some detail in subsequent chapters. However, a return visit to the hypothetical classroom six months later would reveal some dramatic changes.

The children, as they learn to work independently and responsibly, are carefully observed by the teachers who are freed from their traditional place at "the head of the class". The teachers can then move about, helping individual children, checking work, raising a question, giving a word of encouragement, or providing guidance to a small group of children who may be working on a joint project.

Starting Points

The curriculum, rather than being conceptualized as a ladder of sequenced steps, or a series of content units to be mastered, may best be compared with a web, with many points of entry and a network of interconnected areas of interest. The "starting point" may be something in which the child is interested or curious about - or it may be some material or piece of apparatus in the school - it may be a suggestion or demonstration by the teacher - or something another child is doing. With skillful guidance by the teacher, the initial point of investigation may be linked to other related areas of study and, eventually, to the expression of observations and discoveries, using a variety of modes and media.

For example, a discussion about pets and the animals in school one morning offered an interesting starting point. The children talked about their own pets and the hamsters and fish in school. The teacher posed some questions for the children to ponder, not to be answered immediately. The children soon added their own queries for the group to consider. Which of our two hamsters is bigger? Which one weighs more? What do they like to eat? How much? How do the fish breathe? Why do we have to change the water? How do our pets keep clean? Why do the babies sleep so much? How can we find out all these things?

The activity which followed continued for several weeks, rising and waning, and then rising again in new forms. Their investigations were sometimes moved forward by a question from a teacher. "What do you think would happen if...?" Sometimes, their quest was aided by material found in the library; sometimes through the interaction of older and younger children.

Their activities may be documented in the form of a flow chart or diagram: (See Diagram).

Structure

Three elements were required for structuring these open-ended learning situations:

1. The children had to take an active part in their own learning. They had to do something...observe, measure, compare, improvise, experiment, etc.

2. The children had to record what they found. They had to find ways to communicate what they did, what they found out, and what they thought and felt

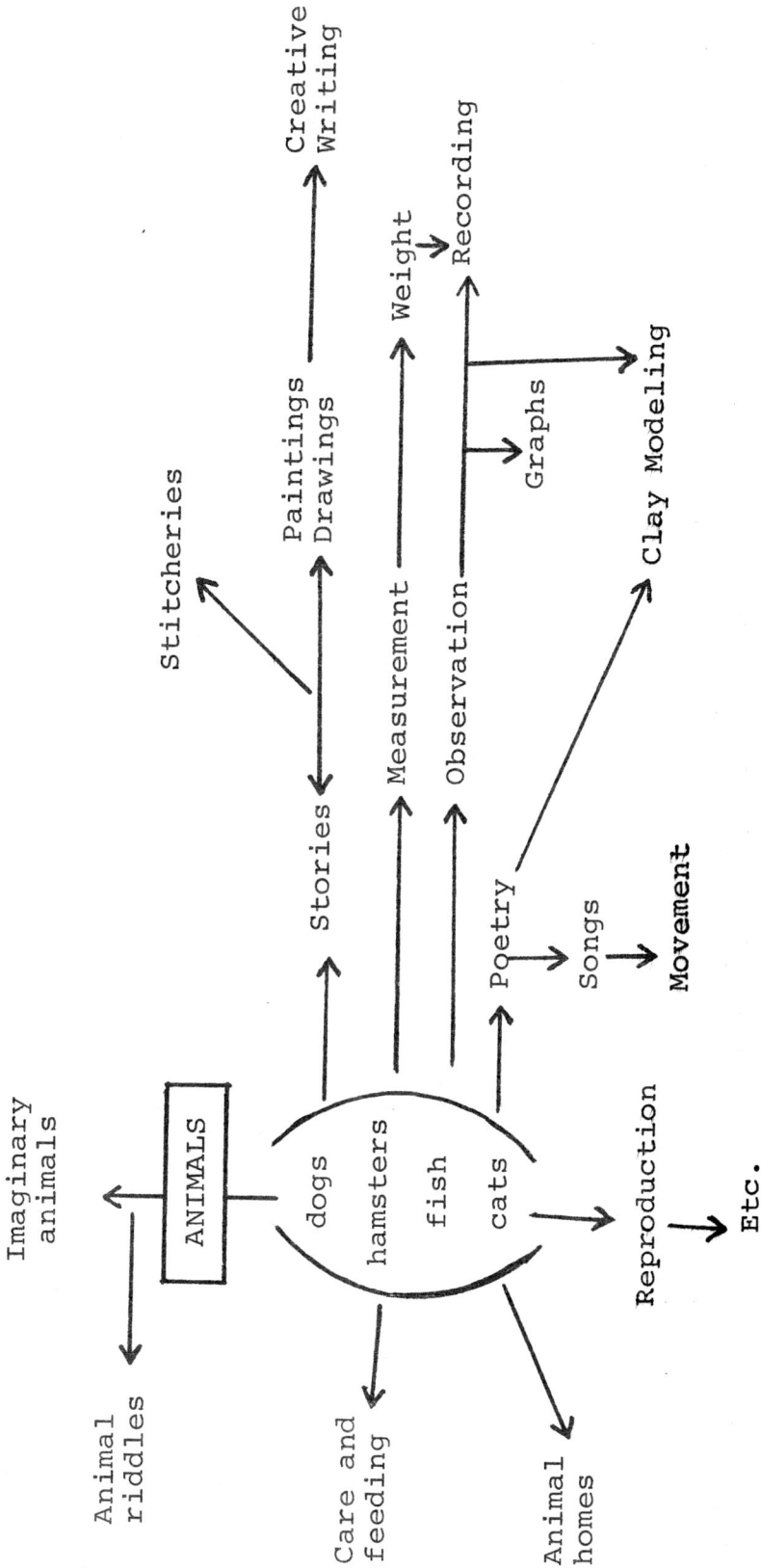

ANIMALS

dogs
hamsters
fish
cats

Imaginary animals → Animal riddles

Care and feeding

Animal homes

Reproduction → Etc.

Stitcheries

Stories

Paintings Drawings → Creative Writing

Measurement → Weight → Recording

Observation

Graphs

Clay Modeling

Poetry → Songs → Movement

about it. This could be done in many ways - by writing, or telling or painting, etc.

3. The tasks had to be defined by the teachers in ways which would permit a wide range of responses, from children with minimal skills to those who were quite sophisticated.

In this instance, those children who could write began to produce stories and poems about their pets or those in school. Their writing had a spontaneous quality.

"The hamster is brown and white. It shakes when it moves. Its food is sunflower seeds and ground corn and ground wheat, ground oats, barley and pellets."

"I have a cat. Her name is Heidi. She is gray and black and wet because she goes in the toilet."

"My kitten is white all over and has tortoise shell splotches on her coat. She lives all over our house and she usually sleeps on my bed at night. I feed her every day after I wake up. She is part Persian, part Siamese and part Angora. She is medium wide and two feet two inches long. That is my kitten."

Some children chose to spend time in careful observation and then recorded what they found interesting or significant. Others read or listened to stories about pets, sang songs about animals and created dances. Of those who had not yet learned to write, some began to want to learn how and were given help in doing so. Others chose to paint, draw and model animals of clay. A few children carried out their ideas in stitcheries.

While many of the starting points came from the children's interests and curiosities, the teachers provided some of them through the informal use of task cards which carried open-ended assignments. These could be in any subject area. A few examples:

"How many ways can we say 30? 5+5+5+5+5+5, 5x6..."

"Make up a secret code and write a message using it. Find a friend who will try to read it."

"Find one person who is taller and one who is shorter than you are. Is there someone who is just as tall as you? Write about it or draw or paint what you find out."

"Draw a picture using only straight lines. What does it make you think of? Write about it."

One of the responses to the last assignment was an interesting drawing and the following piece of creative writing:

"I made a picture with just lines. It is amazing what you can do with just lines. This picture to me looks like the sun on a very sunny day. It also looks like a tree in the summer. It looks like a star, in a way - like the hair of my dog. It looks like jungle grass."

Another child made a survey of attitudes toward reading and recorded the findings in a colorful and attractively mounted graph, with the following explanation:

"I wanted to know how many people like to read. This graph shows what I found out. I found that 13 people in the older group like to read. Five people in the older group don't like to read. In the younger group, 12 people like to read and two don't like to read.

How many people did I question?	32
How many like to read?	−25
How many don't like to read?	7"

This is also an example of the integration of language arts and mathematics in one activity.

Some of the choices the children made were self-initiated and grew out of their own inner needs. One child, for example, when asked by the teacher what she was going to do one morning, responded, "My handwriting is just terrible. I'm going to practice so that when I grow up, I won't write scribble-scratch like my Daddy."

Another child made a booklet titled, "My Poem Book...Big Poems...small poems...HUGE POEMS." It contained writing such as this:

The Mist

The mist comes swirling in
Over hill and lake and city.
The mist comes in on padded feet,
Now it's clear and now it's misty,
You never see it, never hear it
Until it's all around you,
And you are lost in the swirling mist.

The Stars

The stars are always twinkling bright
But only in the night,
But only in the night.
The stars are always scattered, scattered,
The stars are always scattered in the night sky.

The latter poem, when read aloud to a small group of children, demonstrated such a lyrical quality that they suggested it should be set to music. A few children with recorders and music paper went off and fashioned a melody which they later shared with everyone.

Impetus for Change

The climate and the activities of this composite informal classroom differ dramatically from the conventional one. Teachers, parents and administrators who are inclined in this direction frequently ask, "What can we do to move our school toward this approach?"

The impetus for change can come from many sources. In England, it came from the primary teachers and the heads or principals of the small schools which were re-organized after World War II. In the United States, it stemmed from the popular press which reported the sweeping and fundamental changes in the British Primary Schools. Most often, change was begun when parents and teachers and administrators joined together in an effort to reformulate their schools.

For change to occur, there must first be a willingness to examine critically the status quo. One segment of the school - community might light the spark, but all three - teachers, admin-

istrators and parents - must unite in order to begin the process
of change.

CHAPTER 2

LOOKING AT CHILDREN

Informal classrooms reflect theories of child development
and learning theories that are both very old and very new. Many
of the central educational ideas have been espoused by learning
theorists for a century or more but have only received new
importance from the findings of modern research in the cognitive
development of children. Although the theories and research are
complex and not easy to describe briefly, they do suggest that
"traditional" methods of schooling young children are inappropriate and inadequate in many ways. Other educational methods
can be devised which are more in harmony with the nature of
children and the ways in which they learn.

The Child as a Learner

Philosophers and scientists have been looking at children
for a long time. We have come a long way from treating children
as if they were miniature adults. It is not the purpose of this
chapter to re-trace the history of educational thought. Rather,
the focus will be on an examination of contemporary educational
and psychological theories and research. Concern with the nature
of children's learning has been most influenced by Montessori,
Dewey, Piaget, and Bruner. Contributions are still being made by
Piaget and Bruner, as they continue to develop and refine their
work.

In some ways, as Taylor (1972) documented, the work that
has been done overlaps and entwines, showing mutual influence.
According to Piaget, humans progress from simple sensorimotor
conceptions through a series of developments that culminate in
abstract reasoning powers of a high order. (Piaget, 1950, 1954,
1962, 1967). Many psychologists have repeated Piaget's experi-

ments and confirmed his results. (Flavell, 1963; Issacs, 1955).

Piaget the scientist is complemented by Piaget the philosopher who seeks logical systems with internally consistent explanations for all their parts. Piaget proceeds with the assumption that a detailed investigation of any small sample of a species will yield basic information inherent to all members of that species. Having developed a theoretical framework of his own, Piaget's research after 1939 shows a consistent increase in the number of subjects used for the testing of each new hypothesis. His research in the past decade has involved approximately 1500. (Maier, 1969). There had to be a flow of translations to the United States and a great number of Piaget's findings had to be verified by independent psychologists in the United States in order that educational applications could be made.

Various experimenters repeated a great number of Piaget's experiments and then confirmed his results--not only about number but space, time, measurement, volume, etc.

Piaget's theories as applied to early childhood education stress maturation. He does not study differences in environments but common stages and laws of all children's mental growth. There is no denial of influences of environmental factors or of mental growth as resulting from inward maturation. Piaget's whole psychology rests on the principle of continuous interaction between the child and the world around him; it is this that furnishes all the material, as well as the motivating force for his intellectual advance.

As a researcher in human development, Piaget believes that cognitive development rests upon a chain of assumptions:

1. There is a single unity of all things, biological, social and psychological.
2. There are growth points to all mental processes.
3. Human personality evolves from a composite of intellectual and affective functions and from the inter-relation of these two functions. (Maier, 1969).

Piaget's important contribution to child study is the order of succession of distinct developmental phases. These phases serve as convenient descriptive ways to present cognitive development. Six generalizations are included to summarize Piaget's concept of development:

1. There is an absolute continuity of all developmental processes.

2. Development proceeds through a continuous process of generalizations and differentiation.

3. This continuity is achieved by a continuous unfolding. Each level of development finds its roots in a previous phase and continues into the following one.

4. Each phase entails a repetition of processes of the previous level in a different form of organization (schema). Early behavior patterns are replaced by higher order behaviors. (Piaget in Tanner & Inhelder, 1956).

5. The differences in process levels create a hierarchy of experience and actions.

6. Individuals achieve different levels within the hierarchy, although ". . . there is in the brain of each individual the possibility for all these developments but they are not all realized." (Piaget, 1950).

The application of Piaget's theories to informal education blend well with the work of an Italian pediatrician, Maria Montessori (1870-1952). They both have a biological orientation toward the thought and behavior of the child. They both see mental growth as an extension of biological growth and as governed by the same principles and laws. Also, both Piaget and Montessori emphasize the normative aspects of child behavior and development. These aspects of normal development are the starting points for an understanding of differences between individuals. (Flavell, 1963; Montessori, 1964).

The ideas of these two thinkers converge in the nature-nurture interaction. Both see mental growth as an extension of physical growth. Their position means that the environment provides nourishment for the growth of intellect as it does for the growth of physical organs. Therefore, both Piaget and Montessori recognize and take account of the directive role which the environment takes in the determination of mental content.

The young child is considered to have needs and capacities that are quite different from those of the adult, therefore Maria Montessori and Jean Piaget attach considerable importance to the great role which repetitive behavior plays in mental growth. They view mental growth as analogous to physical growth.

It is important to accept the theories of Piaget and Montessori as they were developed and not force their ideas into our existing conceptual frameworks, or distort them for our own pragmatic purposes. (Elkind, 1969). They help to clarify the child-centered developmental approach to education expressed in its broadest form by the American philosopher John Dewey.

As Director of the School of Education at the University of Chicago, John Dewey first began to experiment with his beliefs concerning the philosophy and psychology of education. As a pragmatist, Dewey rejected the authoritarian and classical approach to education which he thought stressed the ability to talk about things rather than the ability to do things. He, along with Montessori and Piaget built his philosophy on a biological base. Dewey thought things were to be understood through their origin and function. The key word in Dewey's child-centered education is growth, the growth of the child in every aspect of his development--physical, moral, intellectual, aesthetic--all directed to the point when all his potentialities for health development have been identified. A second point of importance is the connection in the relationship between education and development. The child-centered teacher believes that the educational process, far from being something which is externally imposed upon a child, must stem from the very nature of development itself. As part of the growth and maturation process, a child passes through a series of developmental stages of growth. Not only must his education be linked to these, it must be founded upon the special nature of each of these stages. From such a relationship between education and development stem our psychological conceptions of the link between interest and motivation, the relevance of the educational experiences to the child's own experience, and the selection of matter and method in

17

accordance with his age, ability and aptitude. (Dewey, 1913).

In the introduction to *Beyond the Information Given*, (Bruner, 1973) the various stages of Bruner's thought and research are summarized. Like Piaget and Dewey, Bruner believes that the child is required to be the active agent of his own learning and that the learning activities must be matched to the developmental stage of the child.

If we accept Piaget's work as valid, then the primary years must be engaged in real living and real learning. Adding to the three R's, we may consider the three E's--Exploring, Experimenting, and Extending.

The child centered approach not only exemplifies an educational philosophy; it also exemplifies a philosophy of the nature of man and of the society in which he will live. In this sense, child-centered education postulates the kind of society to which an educational system must be committed. Child-centered education, aims at producing individuals with initiative, independence of spirit, and the power to shape the society in which they will live. In the rapid social and economic change which characterizes the world today, social and economic change must be faced and an education system which emphasizes early interest in problem solving will help to produce adults who will have the ability to make unique contributions to that society.

Seeing the Child - Ways to Begin

Before any implementation can be started, the teacher must have a clear idea of certain critical characteristics of the children. How does the teacher begin to gather this information? The beginning teacher has had some experience in observing children while in college. The experienced teacher usually has a repertoire of developmental expectations.

The observation of a child requires a cluster of specific skills. The observer must learn to narrow the focus of an observation, blocking out all extraneous information. The most common form of observation currently in practice is a global examination of how a child fits into a particular program. A good record of observation should include the activities of an individual child within a particular time framework.

Effective observation has a clear and specific purpose, and the observer records the child's behavior as vividly as possible. The record should indicate where the child is, where he goes, what he does, what he says, and to whom he says it. For example, in observing problem solving situations, the following outline from the Carnegie-Mellon University Children's School may be helpful.

1. When the children try to solve a problem, how do they solve it?

    a. by trial and error?

    b. do they ask an adult to show them how?

    c. do they observe how other children do it, then try by themselves?

    d. other methods?

2. Note the ages of at least two children (for example the youngest and the oldest) and compare the differences in their motor and mental abilities.

3. Watch at least two children and observe specific problems each had to face and classify causes such as:

    a. physical skill limitation

    b. interference by other children or adults

    c. lack of aggression, initiative, or social techniques

    d. verbal limitation.

4. Note problems solved or not solved by the children.

5. Make a generalization about the children's abilities in problem solving, based on the information you have gathered.

Once the behavior is recorded, it is possible for the teacher to analyze and synthesize the information, in order to plan for instruction. Analysis refers to diagnosis, and synthesis suggests that the teacher puts all the pieces of observation together to form a complete picture.

```
                              (1)
                           Selective
                           Observation


Observation for  (5)                    Analysis of
Evaluation                              Observation (2)
                                        (diagnosis)


                                        Developing Performance
                                             Objectives

Learning  (4)
Activity                                         (3)




                    Alternative learning
                    Activities is mastery
                       is not achieved
```

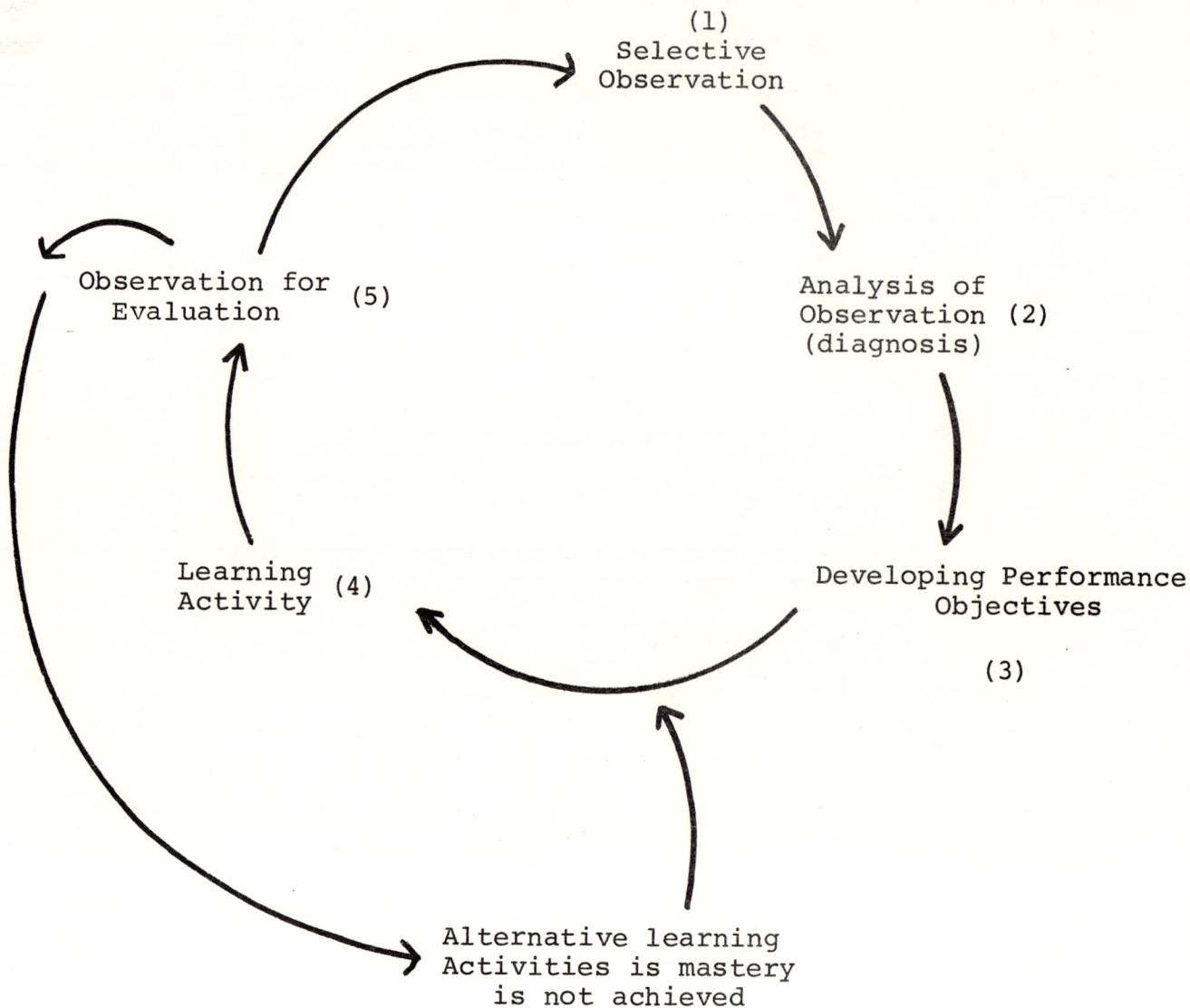

For example, the teacher may not assume that a child has
no physical handicaps unless he verifies vision acuity, hearing
acuity and the absence of speech problems caused by physical dis-
orders. Each of these physical characteristics necessitates
separate assessment.

In a conventional setting, the teacher meets his class

with certain expectations of the children, based on normative data and information from the children's cumulative record cards. In an informal class, the teacher must add another dimension to his early encounters with the children--that of observing the functional level of each individual child. If the class is organized on a cross-age, family grouping or vertical basis, the teacher is compelled to drop grade level expectations and look at each child individually. The teacher of a traditional split class-combined second and third grade, for example, must adopt a mind set that is different from that of a second or third grade teacher. In a vertically grouped class, one would expect to find a wide range of teaching materials and frequent interactions among children of various ages. The split class conjures up the image of two separate sets of children, each with their own graded material, with little or no interaction across age and grade levels.

The practice in some English Primary Schools of vertical age grouping, that is, giving a teacher a class of five, six and seven year olds for a period of two or three years offers many benefits. There are three opportunities for children to enter school when they reach the age of five. The teacher having only seven or eight new children has the opportunity to observe each child's performance carefully. The greater the heterogeniety of the children, the greater is the need to individualize observation and planning for instruction.

Teacher A, who is in an established and conventional school with a stable population, frequently plunges into the instructional program at the first or second grade level, by grouping the children according to their cumulative records. Teacher B, on the other hand, who is in a new informal school without immediate access to previous records must postpone grouping until he had had ample opportunity to observe each child. Teacher B is often stuck by the diversity and range of performance demonstrated by the children. The diversity and range may be similar for Teacher A, but it is not so readily apparent. Individual differences are frequently masked by the process of grouping which provides Teacher A with the illusion of homogeneous groups.

Responding to the Child's Needs

Armed with a mind-set that embraces individualized assessment and the desire to meet the needs of each child, the teacher then is required to develop an instructional program which is consistent with his philosophical position. Again, embracing the concept of teaching the child rather than the text, the teacher formulates what it is that each child needs.

The terminology of behavioral objectives has generated antagonism in many educators. Behavioral objectives have carried the connotation that only cognitive performance can be measured. Critics also point to what appears to be a fragmentation of the learning process by breaking down an activity into tiny measurable bits. Yet, there is much to be gained by utilizing this approach to organizing for learning.

In framing objectives, the teacher can attend to both the cognitive and affective development of the children. More importantly, the teacher's focus shifts from "what shall I teach?" to "what do I want the children to be able to do?" Engaging in the process of writing objectives helps the teacher to specify the learning outcomes, which in turn, heightens his confidence in knowing where he is going. The teacher should be able to:

1. differentiate between objectives which are behaviorally stated and those that are not,
2. write objectives in performance terms for his own particular students,
3. select appropriate materials and teaching strategies that will enable him to meet his written objectives,
4. evaluate the effectiveness of the learning materials and experiences as defined by the written performance objectives,
5. assess the level of achievement each child demonstrates based on a performance objective.

School personnel who are unfamiliar or uncomfortable about writing objectives may consult *Behavioral Objectives and Instruction* (Kibler et al, 1970), *Preparing Instructional Objectives* (Mager, 1962), *Behavioral Objectives* (Plowman, 1971), *Toward*

Humanistic Education (**Weinstein and Fantini, 1970**), and *Writing Worthwhile Behavioral Objectives* (Vargas, 1972).

The behavioral objectives lead the teacher and the children toward identifying and selecting the learning activities which will assist them in accomplishing their goals.

CHAPTER 3

LOOKING AT LEARNING

The Nongraded School and Team Teaching

Probably the most hospitable setting for a move to informal education would be the school which has already adopted an organizational plan that is aimed toward increased individualization of instruction. The informal approach may be considered a logical extension of non-gradedness, continuous progress plans and team teaching. It must be said, however, that non-gradedness or team teaching is not a required prerequisite for informal education; it may merely make the transition easier.

Many educators viewed these organizational changes as holding great promise for the solution of many complex problems facing the school. Traditionally, in the elementary school, six year olds entered first grade where they were expected to master a fixed and pre-determined body of knowledge and skills in order to pass on to the second grade. Those children who did not achieve mastery - or achieved only partial mastery - were either passed on to the next grade level, where their learning problems were compounded, or held back to repeat the year.

Numerous studies demonstrated that retention in grade or repetition of a year had little or no positive effect on the child's achievement and rather negative effects on his self-concept, his social adjustment and his attitudes toward learning. This practice unfortunately still may be found in some of our schools.

The development of the non-graded school represents an effort to acknowledge, in action, the individual needs of each child. This pattern of organization gives active recognition to the spread of ability and readiness which exists at any grade level - a range which may be at least four years in either direction. Further, it acknowledges individual trait differences within each child, i.e. strength in reading skills accompanied by poor concept development in mathematics.

Transforming a traditional graded school into a nongraded one in public school systems has produced its share of problems. In some instances, the only change that occurred was a new set of labels for the classrooms and, perhaps, a new report card format. When a non-graded organization in a school continues to use only graded textbooks and remains bound to a fixed, sequenced curriculum, it produces little change in the quality of education. Non-gradedness, per se, is not enough.

Team teaching, similarly, offers considerable promise for a more effective utilization of teachers' talents, special skills, and interests. It provides greater flexibility for large and small group activity and requires continuous re-grouping of the children according to their achievements. Team teaching, which recognizes individual differences among teachers, and non-gradedness which recognizes individual differences among children, seem to the authors to be natural partners in school organization. But even where both organizational patterns were introduced, the curriculum could still remain relatively unchanged.

Teachers continued to "cover" certain amounts of material within a given period of time and to evaluate progress through the use of standardized achievement tests. For all the grouping and re-grouping which took place, whole class and small group instruction continued, with the teacher rarely having time for individual work with any one child.

Differentiated Staffing

Differentiated staffing refers to the effective, individualized utilization of adults in the school with varying experience, skills and formal training. The number of people involved in such staffing may vary from school to school, depending on the population and the accessibility of the school building.

There is no single model for optimal staffing.

One approach may be characterized by a team leader, sometimes called the group leader or the pod leader, who is usually experienced and skillful in planning with others. The leader must be willing and able to assume the instructional leadership role of the group. He would also serve as the liaison between the staff and the administration. He may, on occasion, participate with staff in conferences with supervisors and parents. The leader may coordinate and facilitate the acquisition and distribution of materials and equipment.

The team or group usually includes a number of experienced certified teachers. In some instances, they may have particular strengths in one or more content area. This not only provides the children with good learning experiences, but the specialist-teacher may assist his colleagues to upgrade their own skills in that content area. The experienced teachers assume the responsibility for identifying and requesting the most recent and the most effective teaching materials for subject areas. Team members work cooperatively not only with the team leader but with other members of the group, sharing time, space and materials. Unlike the conventional classroom, where one teacher is responsible for the 30 children in it, in an effective team operation, all the teachers assume responsibility for all the children in the group. Teachers develop ways of keeping track of academic progress. They share their findings in conferences with the children, parents, and other school personnel.

A team may include a new teacher or two who may be gradually and supportively inducted into the profession. This may prove to be a less traumatic beginning than most solitary placements in the conventional school. Some teacher preparation colleges are beginning to prepare teachers for team teaching situations.

A somewhat recent addition to the staffing is the paraprofessional or teacher aide. Frequently, the aide is a member of the community and a parent of children in the school. The aide may be on a career ladder leading to teacher certification. In the beginning, aides were employed primarily to perform non-teaching duties such as moving audio-visual equipment, collecting lunch money and running the ditto machine. More recently, however, aides are seen listening to a child read or taking a group of children out to recess. Skillful professionals enable the aides to function comfortably and effectively.

As recently as ten years ago, parents were not particularly welcome in the classrooms, except for special occasions. As closer school-community relationships develop, parents as volunteers are beginning to play an increasingly important role in the life of the classroom. By taking a small group of children for an experience in cooking, carpentry or stitchery, they free the professionals to provide more individualization for the other children. Providing real help in the classroom frequently serves to increase the parents' self-esteem. They may also serve an important public relations role in communicating with others in the community.

It has been our experience at Chatham College and Carnegie-Mellon University in Pittsburgh, Pennsylvania that college students, working in classrooms in England, in urban settings, and in rural Appalachia, have been able to make significant and enriching contributions to the growth of children. They can work on a one-to-one basis with a child, help with small group instruction, or with field trips. Some students may bring special skills to the classroom, such as creative dramatics, dance or puppetry. One student in the Elementary Education program at Chatham College, who was majoring in Economics, developed teaching units in that content area for kindergarten children.

Beginning the Transition

The informal classroom may embrace the principles of team teaching, non-gradedness and differentiated staffing and may carry the education process one step closer to the ideal of individualized, personalized, humanistic education.

Making the transition from traditional school activities to an informal classroom approach presents an array of problems and difficulties which should not be minimized. The most obvious and essential prerequisite for change in a public school system is the commitment to this philosophy of education by the building principal, the teachers and the parents. Without the active administrative support and leadership of the principal, and the readiness of the teachers and parents, effective change is not possible.

Brown and Precious (1969) offer the following cautionary advice:

> "There is a danger in moving too quickly into the integrated situation without real understanding and thorough preparation...it is essential that each individual teacher is at a stage where this represents a possible and not too difficult step in her own evolvement...Teachers cannot change overnight. For the change to be sincere and effective it must develop through the teacher's own personal evolvement." (p. 121-123).

Another difficulty in implementing the informal education philosophy lies in the fact that there is no single model which may be replicated. While informal classrooms are based on the same set of principles and assumptions, they vary widely in practice as a function of differences in the personality, character, ability, style, and culture of the school personnel, the children and the community. This is confirmed in the Interim Report of the Educational Testing Service.

Chittenden, et al. (1970) which states,

> "...no single set of administrative rules can be considered to define the British Infant School approach. Contrary to some published accounts, an "open" school may or may not integrate ages, and classrooms may or may not be self-contained ...Another consequence of the..."non-model" is that there tends to be no single expert or authority on it." (p. 11)

Each school, then, is required to develop its own definition, its own formulation, and its own mode of implementation, in terms of the strengths and needs of its constituents. In many ways, this would appear to be a more effective method of change than the more traditional issuance of a mandate or directive which usually emanates from the Central Administrative Office.

It is in the very process in which the school staff must engage, as it develops its own unique definition and formulation, that the seeds of possible success are sown. No single pattern of organization can be expected to meet the needs of a variety of schools, and no one but the participants of a school-community can better define those needs.

Family Grouping

In a school which features team teaching, or is moving in that direction, the teams may be designated as preschool (ages 3 to 5), primary (ages 5 to 8), and intermediate (ages 8 to 10 and 11 to 12). Traditional age-grouping places all five year olds in one classroom, six year olds in another, etc.

Family grouping or vertical age grouping is an alternative which deserves some examination. Vertical age grouping in a school building may result in several classes of five, six and seven year old children, several classes of eight, nine and ten year olds, and several classes of eleven and twelve year olds. This arrangement provides a two or three year period during which a strong rapport and understanding may be developed between teachers and children.

There are several advantages to family grouping. At the beginning of the school year, for example, the teacher of five, six and seven year olds may lose some of the seven year olds who are ready to move into the next older group of eight, nine and ten year olds, and receive a small group of beginning five year olds. The new children entering school for the first time are welcomed into an established class of children who are already familiar with the life of the classroom. (Ridgeway and Lawton, 1968).

> "...the teacher is herself not called upon to get to know, or to consider the needs of 30 to 40 new children all at once, or to build up her classroom atmosphere from scratch each year...There is always a group of experienced children to guide the others; routine tasks are performed more quickly and easily, and time is saved." (p. 19-21)

Another advantage of family grouping is that it permits and encourages peer teaching and learning of academic and social skills. Older children who have already developed responsibility, initiative and independence transmit these qualities to the younger ones.

Greater flexibility is available through family grouping for meeting individual needs, for allowing children to find their own level, and providing for temporary regressions or the fluctuation of interests. Teachers and parents have greater opportunity to develop sound relationships when the child remains with the same teacher for two or three years.

In choosing between the traditional horizontal age grouping and family grouping, it is clear that either approach presents advantages and disadvantages which, again, must be weighed and evaluated by the school and the community in terms of their own particular needs.

The Integrated Day

The integrated day, that is, the school day which is not interrupted by arbitrary time divisions or periods, and which is characterized by a flow from one activity to another, can be approached in a number of ways. It will develop neither automatically nor instantly, but may reflect varying stages of a developmental process. Time will be required to permit both teachers and children to unlearn old, established routines and to develop their own unique ways of living and working together in the classroom.

In a self-contained classroom, the teacher may choose to continue to plan directed small-group instruction for part of the day, setting aside one or two periods for exploratory independent activities. Another option may be found in substituting independent activity in the learning centers for the traditional seat work. The maintenance of small-group instruction, especially in the beginning stages, will provide for a sense of continuity, familiarity and stability during the transition to new patterns.

Teachers, parents and administrators may find comfort and reassurance in the fact that the basic skills of literacy and number are still being attended to in an orderly and systematic fashion while new activities are being introduced. Later, as alternative approaches to instruction in skills are developed, they may then encounter less resistance.

Changes in the quality of life in the classroom must evolve gradually over time. The processes of change cannot and should not be hurried. A great deal of careful thought and planning is required in the early stages of implementation, and ideally, the classroom teacher should be able to move at a rate and in a style comfortable to him, and have ample access to support and consultation.

There are probably as many starting-points as there are teachers. One teacher may want to begin by introducing one learning center, such as reading and language arts where the children may find an assortment of supplementary readers, trade books, word building games, language games, writing materials, activity cards, etc. He will carefully explain to the whole class how and when this center may be used. He will avoid putting out too much material at once, and will rotate the materials in order to maintain high interest among the children.

Another teacher may be sufficiently experienced and confident to open two or three learning centers at once, providing the children with both the opportunity for independent activity and the additional dimension of making responsible choices.

Preparing to make the transition from the conventional to the informal may be viewed in stages or levels of activity. Taylor (1971) suggests five stages. Stage I would be concerned with three main tasks: grouping the children, training them in the use of materials and in class organization, and establishing discipline and control. Grouping assists in the introduction of informal education, and later, in the maintenance of the organization.

"The success of an Integrated Day will stand or fall by the children's ability to act independently, to make decisions, and to help themselves. Teacher-direction in its obvious form cannot recede into the background until the children have been trained to fill the gap which it appears to leave." (p. 61)

31

The most careful preparation and the best organizational plans can be defeated by inadequate or ineffective control and discipline. This may sound contradictory or paradoxical to the philosophy of informal education, but as Taylor (1971) has said:

> "'Controlled freedom', in which each child can satisfy his own needs without thereby preventing others from doing the same, is important enough to delay any move toward integration until the teacher is confident that she can handle the class without undue strain. When she knows that she can allow freedom without license, and variety of purpose without confusion, she is safe in assuming that she can extend the children's responsibility without fear of the consequences." (p. 62)

By the end of the first stage, the children should be able: to work in groups and individually in constructive and responsible ways, to get the materials they need and put them away when they are finished, to exercise a measure of self-discipline in managing their own behavior, and to move from one task to the next without constant dependence on the teacher's direction.

The second stage introduces the beginnings of the integrated day. The teacher may retain the traditional teacher-directed activity for all but one hour. During that one hour, the teacher may specify two tasks for each group, leaving to the children the choice of the order in which they will do them. A third supplementary task may be set for those children who complete both tasks quickly.

The remaining stages gradually expand the amount of time during which the children make choices and work independently. The tasks specified by the teacher may, when necessary, include some time for direct instruction of a group or part of a group of children, in order to enable them to move to the next stage of their learning. As Taylor (1971) has said:

> "Plans must allow for direct teaching in the same way as they allow for any other activity, and this becomes particularly important as the period of integrated work is lengthened. There is nothing about an Integrated Day which makes direct teaching

any less essential than it has always been in a
programme organized on traditional lines."
(p. 71)

It is perhaps around the issue of direct instruction, and
its place in informal education, that controversy exists. There
are those educators who believe that teacher-directed activities
and direct instruction are antithetical to the philosophy of informal education, and that children must have total choice to "do
their own thing."

To adopt that extreme position, the writers feel, would be
an abdication of the teacher's responsibility. In an informal
classroom, the teacher continues to be responsible for creating
an exciting and inviting learning environment, and for the provision of appropriate choices for the children. To do otherwise
would be to invite chaos and anarchy.

CHAPTER 4

MAKING IT WORK

The movement toward informal education may take a variety of routes, depending on the individual situation in which it is to occur. For example, in an urban school system, the directive to change may emanate from a central administrative office. Different strategies may be required than those employed in a school district where the initiative may originate with the building principal.

In an urban neighborhood, where parents are well-read in contemporary education literature, the parents may be the source of persuasion for the school to move toward the informal approach. Where new housing is being constructed, in suburban areas, parents and school boards may be searching for new and better ways to implement effective learning for their children.

A group of teachers in a school building may be the source of the impetus for change. Although individual teachers may want to alter their teaching approach, it is virtually impossible for a teacher to do it alone. Both in England and in the United States, we continually encounter teachers who say, emphatically, that they could not have made the change without the help and support of colleagues.

Sometimes, university and college professors have been able to collaborate successfully with school districts, in order to provide alternative settings for undergraduate and graduate students who are preparing to become teachers. In these situations, college faculty with their students have functioned as agents of change, helping school personnel to move toward individualization of instruction.

In some instances, State Departments of Education have been instrumental in bringing together school districts and university personnel for the purpose of reformulating the educational system, based on current research findings in child development and learning theory.

Organization

Perhaps the most important dimension of an effective informal program is careful organization. This is crucial, not only in the initial phases, but re-examination of organizational practices must continue throughout the school year. Flexibility is the chief goal of a good organizational pattern. Teachers must be encouraged to discard nonfunctional elements and to design new ones which will facilitate and enhance learning activities.

There is no blueprint for organization. It must grow naturally from a series of dialogues among the school personnel, as they identify and define their long-range objectives. These objectives should be articulated in written form for several reasons: a) They can then be shared with parents, board members, visitors and others; b) They can be re-examined periodically for confirmation or revision as to their validity; c) The very process of putting them into written form makes demands for clarification of thinking; d) They will be instrumental in the process of evaluation.

Planning and Management

A popular romantic view of informal education assumes that bringing children and loving adults together in an interesting environment will automatically create a good learning situation. This "airy-fairy" approach is most frequently found in the precious, private "free" schools and, to the writers, it leaves much to be desired. It is too dependent on spontaneity and incidental learning and too casual about defining goals and preparing the environment.

Just as the informal approach does not abandon the practice of defining its objectives, neither does it abandon the need for lesson plans, for order and for discipline. The difference lies in the nature of the planning, and the development of self-discipline which it encourages.

Similarly, the acquisition of skills is not to be left to chance in the informal classroom. It is not so much the "what" of children's learning which changes as it is the "how".

For example, in a good informal classroom, children are led to discover their need for particular skills in order to solve problems. Rather than teaching phonics, as such, or rules about grammar, children are helped to formulate generalizations which they can then apply in a variety of situations. The skillful teacher will also recognize when the child is ready for stretching and will provide motivation which will lead him to increasingly higher order skills.

Time for planning in an informal school occurs throughout the day, as teachers and others encounter each other. This is, in part, another reflection of an educational philosophy in action which encourages cooperative planning. This is in contrast to more conventional settings where the planning is done centrally and teachers are viewed as the "message bearers".

The principal can be instrumental in providing blocks of time for planning through his use of specialists in the building, and with team teaching. In some schools, it is an accepted practice to dismiss the children early on a regularly scheduled basis to allow additional planning time.

There are a variety of starting points which teachers may consider in beginning to plan an informal program. These include: field trips, children's interests, teachers' interests, listening to children's conversations, referral to curriculum guides, textbooks and trade books, professional journals and instructional material.

Planning is usually easier and more effective if the thematic approach is employed. This will be discussed more fully later in the chapter.

There are several basic elements of good management practice. These elements will evolve, as teachers and children plan and grow. Depending on the individual situation, it may take weeks, months, even years, before they are stabilized.

1. Materials should be stored systematically and should

be easily accessible to the children. The teacher's inventory should enable him to project the needs of the classroom. Materials should be rotated periodically in order to maintain high levels of interest and motivation.

Teacher-made materials should be sturdy and durable. The selection and purchase of materials should be focused on flexibility of use.

2. It is the teacher's responsibility to create an aesthetically pleasing environment in which learning can take place. This is a necessity either in a new open-space building or a conventional self-contained classroom.

    The teacher will have to provide space for whole class needs as well as for individual children's needs. This includes a secluded place for quiet activities, ample opportunity for privacy and clearly demarcated learning areas.

3. The teacher must create the methods and the devices which will enable the children to assume the responsibility for managing the taking of attendance, basic housekeeping tasks, choice of learning activities and keeping records.

    There are unlimited ways of doing these things. The following are just a few arbitrary examples.

Attendance:

September	10	11	12	13	14
John	x	x	x	x	
Sue	x			x	
Ellen	x		x	x	

This can be a simple wall-chart with a crayon tied to a piece of yarn. Children can check themselves in when they come to school.

It may be done in a seasonal shape each month--a large leaf for
September, a pumpkin for October, etc.

	4	5	6	7	8
Mary	x		x		
Alice	x	x	x		
Jerry	x		x		
Sally		x	x		
Jim	x	x	x		

March

Housekeeping tasks may be designated on a flannel board. Symbols
for the task may be cut out of felt. Name tags for the children
may be made of oak tag with a piece of felt glued to the back.

```
┌─────────────────────────────────────────────────────┐
│   🌻        HELPERS                                   │
│   ▣                                                  │
│              Mary                                    │
│   ✂                                                  │
│              Jim                                     │
└─────────────────────────────────────────────────────┘
```

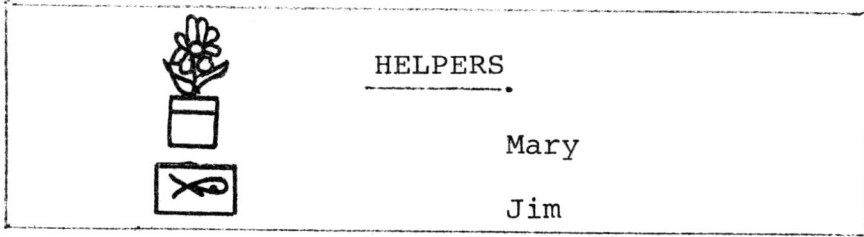

Or it may be done with cut-out hands and picture hangers:

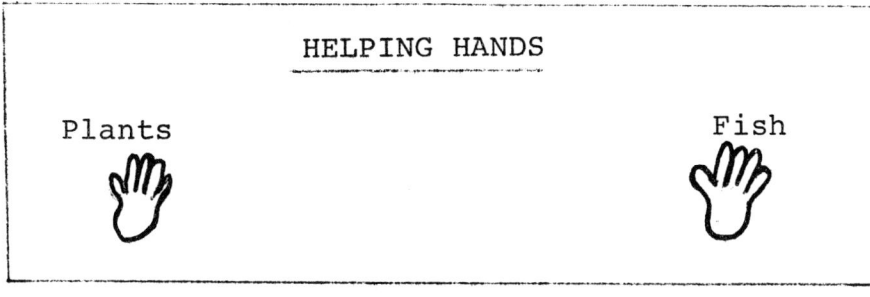

```
┌─────────────────────────────────────────────────────┐
│              HELPING HANDS                           │
│                                                      │
│    Plants                              Fish          │
│      ✋                                  ✋           │
└─────────────────────────────────────────────────────┘
```

For choice of learning activities, a large sheet of pegboard may
be mounted on the wall and painted in stripes with each color
representing a learning center, i.e. pink for social studies,
orange for language arts, etc. The teacher indicates which centers are open and how many children may work in each area. The
teacher may make assignments until the children are sufficiently
mature and ready to do so. Golf tees are inexpensive and available in many attractive colors. They are inserted in the pegboard and the child or teacher hangs on the tee a cardboard disc
with the child's name on it.

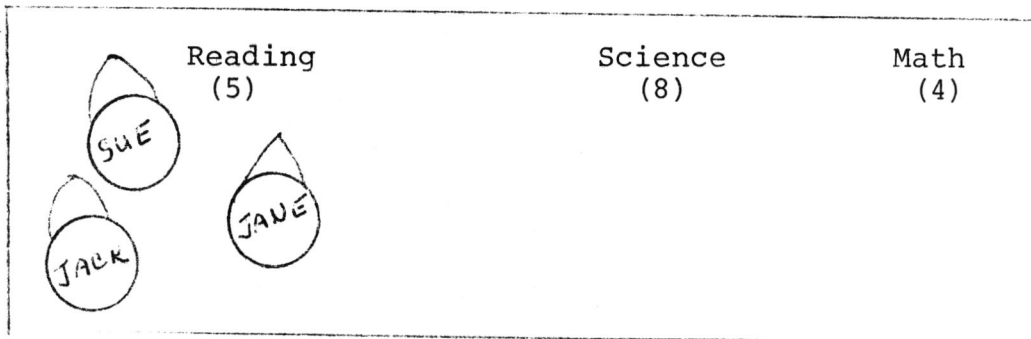

```
┌─────────────────────────────────────────────────────┐
│        Reading          Science          Math       │
│         (5)               (8)             (4)        │
│   SUE                                                │
│   JACK   JANE                                        │
└─────────────────────────────────────────────────────┘
```

Examples of record keeping are to be found in Chapter VI.

4. Floor plans and room arrangements should be done on paper as an initial step. The principal may provide scale drawings of the school to help the teachers in the process.

5. The teacher must develop methods and devices for enabling volunteers to accommodate themselves to the learning program without constant contact with the teacher. This applies to parents, members of the community, pre-service students and aides. A clarifying statement about differentiated staffing was made in Chapter III.

The teacher determines the number of adult helpers he can comfortably utilize. A file box may be kept in the school office with 5 x 8 index cards indicating the location and activity of each volunteer. This also serves as a security measure.

Name tags may be made for each volunteer. This is helpful in identifying people who are in the building on legitimate business.

6. In schools with intercoms, these devices should be used sparingly, perhaps limiting announcements to one brief period during the day.

Traffic Patterns

The movement of children in a classroom and through a school building requires careful pre-planning by the teacher. The design of traffic patterns is one of the "invisible" elements in the structure of an effective informal classroom. While it is difficult to separate patterns of traffic from the consideration of room arrangement, learning centers, etc., the remainder of this section will focus primarily upon planning for mobility.

The teacher's planning and organization are unobtrusive to the children and to the casual observer. The children are often not aware that the teacher, through the "behind-the-scenes"

structuring of the environment, has predetermined where certain
learning activities will occur.

To facilitate the flow of traffic and to provide spaces
for both large and small activities, the teacher must be a
skilled observer of the children and their changing needs. The
teacher must know the approximate size of the children and how
much space they require in both the quiet and active areas. Different types of work need different areas of varying size, i.e.
a place for writing and a woodwork shop. For example, four conventional desks, pushed together, form a large work table surface
which invites small cooperative group activity.

The teacher provides the children with cues which subtly
inform them about how a particular area is to be used. By placing a table and some chairs near the shelves which hold the
manipulative-exploratory math materials, the teacher is, in fact,
saying "Here is a comfortable place to use these materials. This
is where these materials belong."

Attention must be given to traffic patterns throughout the
school. The judicious use of living plants and display areas can
affect the flow of traffic. Placing them near an entrance provides a "go slow" cue to children who will, indeed, slow down and
open the door more carefully.

The beautiful displays in some English Primary Schools are
often initiated by the Head and continued by the staff and, sometimes, the children. Traffic in the halls and on the stairways
can be controlled by carefully placing these displays at strategic
spots.

Within a classroom, the teacher arranges the space in
order to provide for simultaneous activities - a quiet place for
reading and writing, painting and other forms of recording, and
spaces for construction and experimental activities.

As the teacher and the children develop a sense of group
and settle into a social community where people are aware of
each other, the children's movement will express mutual consideration by a decline in rushing, pushing and jostling. Children
will move with greater responsibility as they grow and develop.

The following diagram illustrates the traffic patterns of

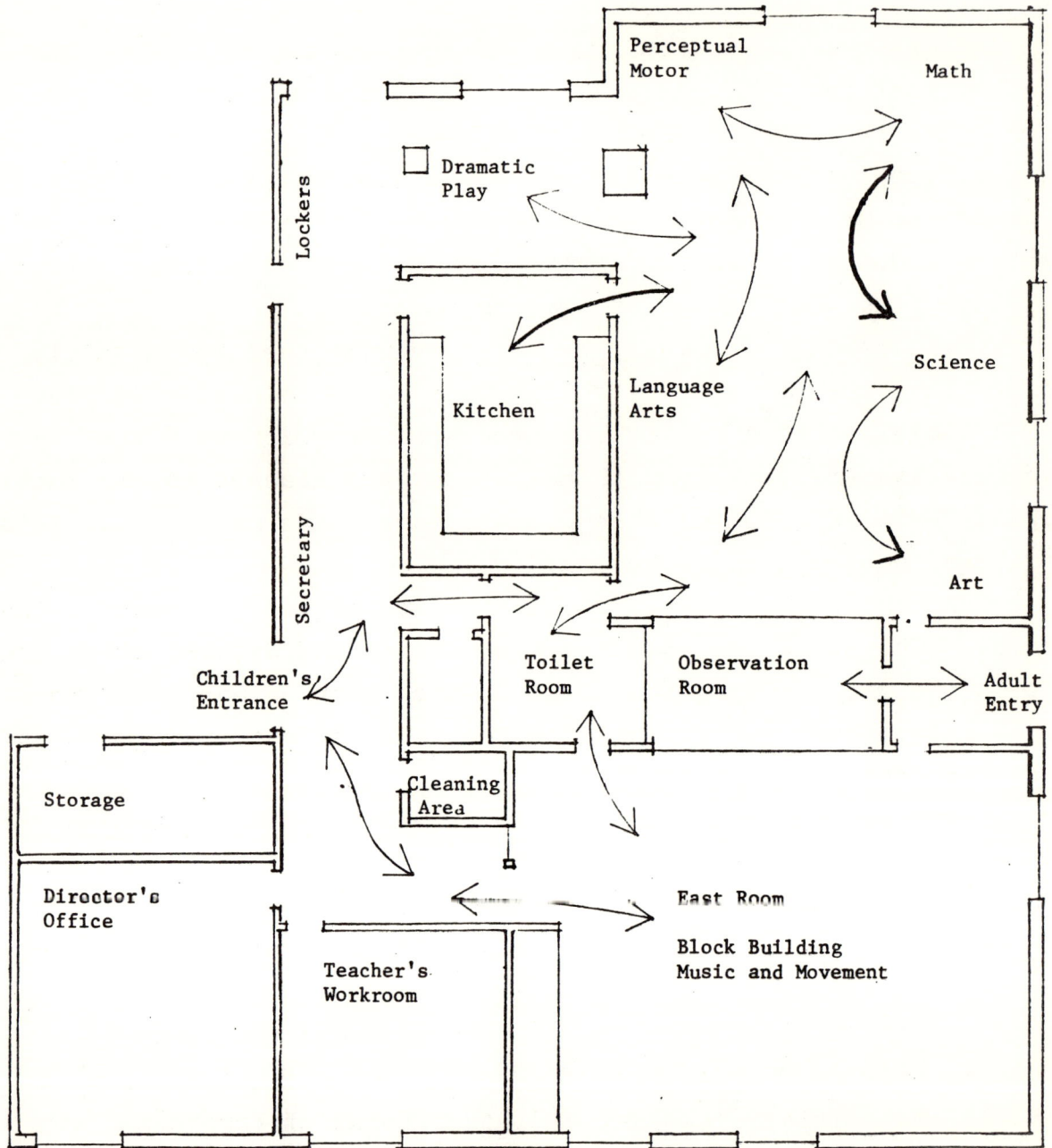

DIAGRAM I

Carnegie-Mellon University
Children's School Design
30 children - traffic patterns

the Children's School at Carnegie-Mellon University, Pittsburgh, Pennsylvania (Diagram I). These rooms were arranged in order to facilitate movement and independence, to encourage interaction between the child and his environment, the child and his peers, and the child and the adults.

Tables are placed near the learning centers in order to facilitate small group activities and instruction. The number of chairs informs the children of how many places are available there. Similarly, in the painting area, the four sides of the two easels indicate that there is room for four painters at one time.

Diagram II is a different design of the same space. This adaptation was made to serve 48 three, four and five year old children. The first design served approximately 30 children. Diagram II also shows the development of the use of corridors.

From time to time, the teacher may want to systematically monitor the movement of children and adults, in order to evaluate existing traffic patterns and to modify them as needed.

Scheduling

Rigid scheduling in some school systems may be a consequence of attempts by administrators and school boards to achieve business-like efficiency in the schools. Efficiency and organization are concepts which school board members, parents, taxpayers and those trained to be administrators can understand and support.

There is some reasonable justification for the development of rigid scheduling in the schools. The majority of children attending school in the United States are transported by bus. Frequently, bus schedules dictate the beginning and ending of the school day. In many school systems, the complexity of transporting children to and from school represents a sizable dollar expenditure. Transportation demands careful planning to coordinate routes and attendance patterns. Planning takes time, and time is also expensive.

School administrators are also faced with the necessity of assuring the public that all the content areas of curriculum are

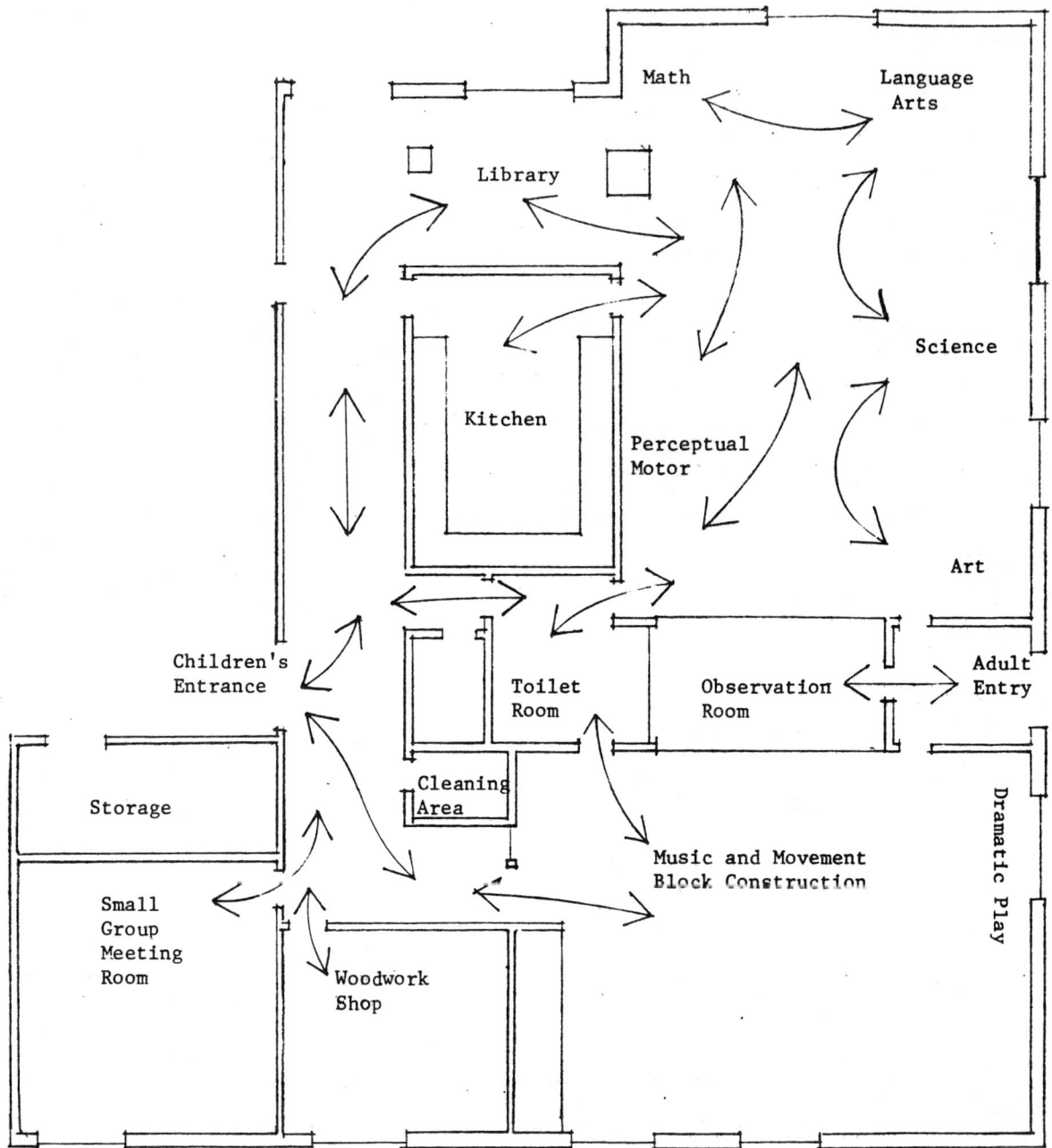

Math

Language
Arts

Library

Science

Kitchen

Perceptual
Motor

Children's
Entrance

Art

Toilet
Room

Observation
Room

Adult
Entry

Cleaning
Area

Storage

Small
Group
Meeting
Room

Music and Movement
Block Construction

Woodwork
Shop

Dramatic Play

DIAGRAM II

Carnegie-Mellon University
Children's School Design
48 Children - traffic patterns

44

adequately "covered". Subdividing the school day into 40 minute time segments, and assigning a subject to each period, demonstrates to the children, teachers and parents that an efficient scheduling procedure is in operation and all subjects are being taught.

Conventional scheduling provides the supervisory and administrative staff the convenience and predictability of what they will encounter when they visit a classroom to observe and evaluate a teacher's performance. In many primary classrooms, a visit between 9:30 and 10:30 in the morning would reveal the teacher engaged with a group of children in reading and language arts activities while the rest of the class worked on workbooks or dittoed work sheets. This predictability also enables the supervisory and administrative personnel to make the most efficient use of their own time.

Scheduling is an important concern for administrators in arranging time for the special teachers of Art, Music, Physical Education, etc. Distribution of the services of the special teachers among the children and teachers requires careful planning. The scheduling of specialist teachers should present no particular difficulty. The integrated day in an informal classroom can easily adapt itself to some scheduling as it becomes necessary. Just as there may be times when whole-class instruction is most appropriate, i.e. in introducing new material or apparatus, so may a specialist French or math teacher be scheduled in for specific periods of time within the broader organizational pattern of the day.

Lunch periods, recess, and teacher preparation time must be considered in the development of an efficient and functional schedule. The schedule may be of help in locating a teacher or a child quickly, because of some emergency.

Consideration of all of these factors can lead one to understand why the complicated and rigid scheduling process has become a way of life in so many schools in the United States. Critics of the schools have said that they are organized for the convenience of the educators, just as hospitals are said to be organized for the convenience of members of the medical profession.

It should be pointed out that time allocations for content areas are frequently suggested by State Departments of Education. Local school administrators sometimes interpret the guidelines as mandates and apply them as such. Schedules should be developed in order to meet the needs of each school community. Most state curriculum guides recommend how much time should be devoted to each subject but rarely are they intended to be definitive.

Alternative ways of scheduling and organizing time must be examined. It may not be possible to ignore bus schedules, but other restrictions should be questioned in order to determine whether they help or hinder in meeting the basic responsibility of the school--teaching children how to learn and to value learning as a life-time activity.

Some Alternative Methods of Scheduling

It is advantageous to consider several options in the process of moving from conventional scheduling toward the integrated day. To assure comfort and security for both teachers and children, change should take place gradually.

One strategy is to plan the initial schedule cooperatively among principals, teachers and ancillary staffs. The principal would be using his leadership role creatively if he confers with the faculty as the first step in planning. There are positive psychological effects for teachers when they are able to share their needs and suggestions which affect the way they invest the hours of their working day. It would be futile to embark on a revised schedule if teachers can see no advantage to either themselves or the children. The inclination may be to adopt a pre-planned model, only to find that it does not meet the teachers' particular needs.

The following charts suggest ways in which rigid scheduling could be modified as a staff moves toward the integrated day. Experience dictates that caution should be used in interpreting the options. Individual schools have unique conditions which influence implementation.

Option I

8:30 - 9:00	Class meeting-plans for the day. Review of previous work. Opportunities for oral communication and development of listening skills.		
	Group A	Group B	Group C
9:00 - 9:30	Direct Reading Instruction	Independent Work	Free choice of options suggested by teacher
9:30 - 10:00	Independent work	Free choice	Direct Instruction
10:00 - 10:30	Free Choice	Direct instruction	Independent work
10:30 - 11:00	Activities such as movement, creative play, puppetry, writing, etc. Recess		
11:00 - 11:30	Math groups		
11:30 - 12:30	Lunch		
12:30 - 1:00	Spelling		
1:00 - 1:15	Handwriting		
1:15 - 1:45	Social Studies		
1:45 - 2:00	Recess		
2:00 - 2:30	Science		
2:30 - 3:30	Special subjects - Art, Music, Physical Education		
3:30 - 3:45	Closing - Evaluation and plans for tomorrow		

Option II

8:30 - 9:00	Class meeting - plan for the day - recap of previous day. Opportunities for oral communication and development of listening skills.
9:00 - 11:30	Two and one-half hour language arts block - reading, listening, speaking, writing, spelling, handwriting, creative dramatics, puppetry, informal music, movement -

```
9:00 -  3:00 Integrated Day

3:00 -  3:45 Closing - evaluation and sharing plans for
                tomorrow.
```

During the primary years, emphasis is generally placed
upon children's acquisition of basic skills. Traditionally, it
is expected that young children will need more direct instruction in the language arts and mathematics than when they reach
the middle grades. Maturity tends to go hand in hand with
children's ability to work independently and to employ the skills
learned in the early years.

Other Ways of Using the School Dollar

This section is not concerned with school finance, as
such, but rather the consideration of alternative ways of utilizing existing funds for the classroom.

Conventionally, most large school districts permit teachers to order supplies from printed lists which limit their
choices. Allowing them to order from supplementary catalogues
would provide greater flexibility and encourage professionalism
on the part of the teachers and would enable them to meet the
particular needs of the children.

There has been a welcome decline in the practice of pur-
chasing 30 identical books for a class. More schools are adopt-
ing multiple texts on a variety of reading levels to meet the
needs of children in terms of maturity, achievement and interest.
There is also a growing trend to spend less money on sophisticated equipment which can only be operated by adults. More is
being spent on hardware which the children can use directly--
film strip projectors, 8mm single concept loops, cassettes, etc.

Video tape equipment and closed circuit TV are valuable
investments and may be used creatively in many ways. Television
may be one way of extending the benefits of team teaching. It
may be used in developing the children's communication skills,
and it has proven itself as an invaluable aid in in-service programs.

When we look at primary schools in England, it is apparent

that with much less money than is spent in the United States, it is possible to develop wholesome environments in which children may flourish. Each school is given a fixed amount of money, depending on pupil population, and each staff and head have the latitude to determine collectively how it is to be spent. This is another opportunity for school personnel to develop and maintain a heightened sense of professionalism.

When an entire school faculty is involved in making decisions about instructional materials, several benefits may result:

a) A school-wide view of existing resources is gained.

b) Individual possessiveness about equipment and apparatus is diminished.

c) Duplication is avoided.

d) Long-range planning is facilitated.

e) Teachers are helped to evaluate prospective materials in terms of quality, durability and flexibility.

f) Individual classroom and school-wide needs and priorities are sorted out and balanced.

Staffing

Perhaps the least effective way to begin is by a central administrative directive which mandates informal education for teachers and principals who may not be ready for it. It would seem that if central office personnel want to provide leadership, they can convene a representative group of teachers, principals and parents to explore the feasibility of change. Central office personnel can provide on-going support by seeking approval from the Board of Education, securing necessary funding, providing in-service education and consultation services, etc.

The major leadership role ultimately rests with the building principal who is charged with altering the climate of his school.

If he accepts this role, he should be given the latitude to select his own staff. The problems facing the principal who has this latitude are quite different from those facing the principal who inherits a faculty.

For those who must deal with an entrenched faculty, change

will be slower and more arduous. It would be helpful for him to survey his staff about their attitudes toward children and learning. This could probably be done most effectively through individual, informal conferences. Group discussions, unless they are very skillfully directed, can lead to polarization and other political problems among the teaching staff. If he can identify a few teachers who are ready for change, he can put his energies into supporting their efforts to begin. In this way, there can soon be an operating demonstration of informal education in the building. If more than one educational approach is to co-exist in a school, extreme caution must be used to avoid a competitive situation.

In our experience, it is usually the threatened or less competent teacher who is resistant to change. A skillful principal will recognize and value individual differences among the teachers and accept them in terms of where they are in their professional development.

The role of parents in staffing a school should be an advisory one. A valuable contribution would be the identification of expected goals for their children.

Teachers who are engaged in an informal school or in informal classrooms in conventional schools must be concerned about physical isolation and professional isolation. This can be minimized by the pairing of teachers (cooperative teaching), team teaching, teacher seminars for sharing ideas, inter-school visits and continuing in-service workshops to meet specific needs.

Representatives of the teaching staff should participate in the selection of new teachers. This is a typical procedure at the college and university level and should be extended downward to the elementary school. This practice would enhance the teachers' sense of professionalism by making them a real part of the decision-making process. It would also diminish the tendency to criticize the hiring practices of principals and central office personnel.

Assuming that a strong partnership can be developed between colleges, universities and school districts, teacher preparation programs can provide skillful human resources to meet staffing needs. Furthermore, as college and university teacher preparation programs become identified as the "producers" of competent beginning teachers for informal classrooms, they can serve the nation's schools in staffing for change. Teacher preparation faculty also represent one of the most valuable resources for designing and implementing effective in-service programs.

Careful consideration of staffing is an important aspect of the development of an informal school. All research points to the teacher as the pivotal feature of any educational approach. New buildings, open space plans, equipment, and instructional materials are important, but the teacher remains at the very heart of the enterprise.

If the informal approach is not a comfortable one for some teachers, they should not be made to feel guilty or inadequate. They should be reassigned to a situation where they can feel successful and competent. The philosophy of staffing which demonstrates genuine concern for the teaching staff is then consistent with the philosophy of informal education.

The movement toward informal education is most likely to occur when there is an effective collaboration among all the constituencies--the school board, administrators, principals, supervisors, teachers and parents, working alongside of college and university faculties.

The Thematic Approach

Organizing instructional units around a theme provides motivation and integration of the curriculum. The thematic approach helps to ensure that all content areas are included, and it brings teachers and children together in the planning process.

The thematic approach assists in moving toward the integrated day. One of the main values of a theme is that it can provide an individual teacher of a differentiated team with a framework for planning. The selection of a topic or theme suggests materials--books, pictures, filmstrips, resource people, and learning activities. It is a strategy for moving away from "teaching the text" and toward a unification of learning.

This approach includes the children in the planning process, in the selection of the theme and in the exploration of it. Children then have the freedom to investigate those aspects of the theme which interests them and may enter it at their individual ability level. It is a way of fostering creativity and of individualizing instruction. It also helps the teacher of a self-contained classroom or the team in a pod to arrange the physical environment in an aesthetically pleasant way. Unlike the conventional classroom, it allows for trait differences and ensures success for each child in some activity.

Research techniques play an important role in relation to the thematic approach. The child must learn alphabetization in order to use the card catalogues in the library. Spelling, rather than involving the rote learning of 15 arbitrarily chosen words, becomes a functional skill, essential to the child who wants to communicate his findings in writing. The teacher guides the child in framing the questions he wants to find out about and offers possible resources for answering his questions.

Today's children, in order to function flexibly and effectively ten years from now, will need to be able to pose questions and seek answers that today's educators cannot predict. Teachers may begin to develop these skills in children by asking questions which only require simple recall and go on, as the children develop, to ask "why" in addition to "what". The questioning process is valuable in helping children to learn to integrate and synthesize what they know.

The writers have observed an inconsistency between theory and practice in some so-called "open classrooms" where programmed instruction is required of all children. Programmed instruction is based on the assumption that all children must pass through a predetermined sequence of activities in order to achieve mastery. Only the rate of learning is individualized and no account is taken of differences in learning style.

There is a place for programmed materials in an informal classroom. It may be suggested by the teacher that a particular child may profit from some experience with programmed instruction materials or a child may choose that type of learning material for himself. The faculty and principal will need to survey available commercial programs in order to select those which are appropriate to the themes being considered.

The thematic approach assists the specialist (Music, Art, etc.) in choosing compatible learning activities. It is also helpful in identifying resource people from the larger community who may be invited to the school. Field trips may add still another dimension.

Not all children should be required to work on all aspects of a theme. As themes change, one child should not always be the one to paint the backdrop of the mural. It is the teacher's responsibility to re-direct learning and to achieve a balance of activity for each child.

Interest in a particular theme may fade over a period of time and resurface later in the year. It can be open-ended and may last for a week or for several months. Branching off in other directions may occur, suggesting a webbing of learning activities. Many activities may be going on simultaneously. For example, when children in the Carnegie-Mellon University Children's School were learning about dinosaurs, they measured off 85 feet in the hall in order to get a concrete experience with size. This led some children into a series of measurement activities which continued for some time.

A theme may provide a life-long interest which will occupy leisure time in the future or give direction in choosing a career.

The informal classroom should provide a comfortable environment where it is safe to take risks. The climate should be supportive. Mistakes are acknowledged and corrected but not penalized. The total atmosphere should be characterized by "What would happen if...?" and "How can we find out?" and "Let's try...".

After a theme has been selected, the teachers and children define their goals and objectives. These may change as the theme is developed, but implementing a theme without goals will not be productive.

For example, if the theme were to be - "The Study of the Community," some broad general goals may

53

include:

The child will be able to:

1. Formulate questions about his community.

2. Use a wide range of resources to gather information--
    the library, human resources, newspapers, TV and the
    community itself.

3. Document and share his findings through improved com-
    munication skills.

Diagram III illustrates some aspects of implementation.
The child may enter the central topic from any of the spokes.

The thematic approach is being used in a growing number
of classrooms. Many teachers find it helpful in making the
gradual transition to the informal classroom. Experienced educators are aware that the thematic approach is not a new way of
organizing the instructional program. However, as the informal
approach requires a fresh and different way of looking at children and learning, the thematic approach deserves re-examination.

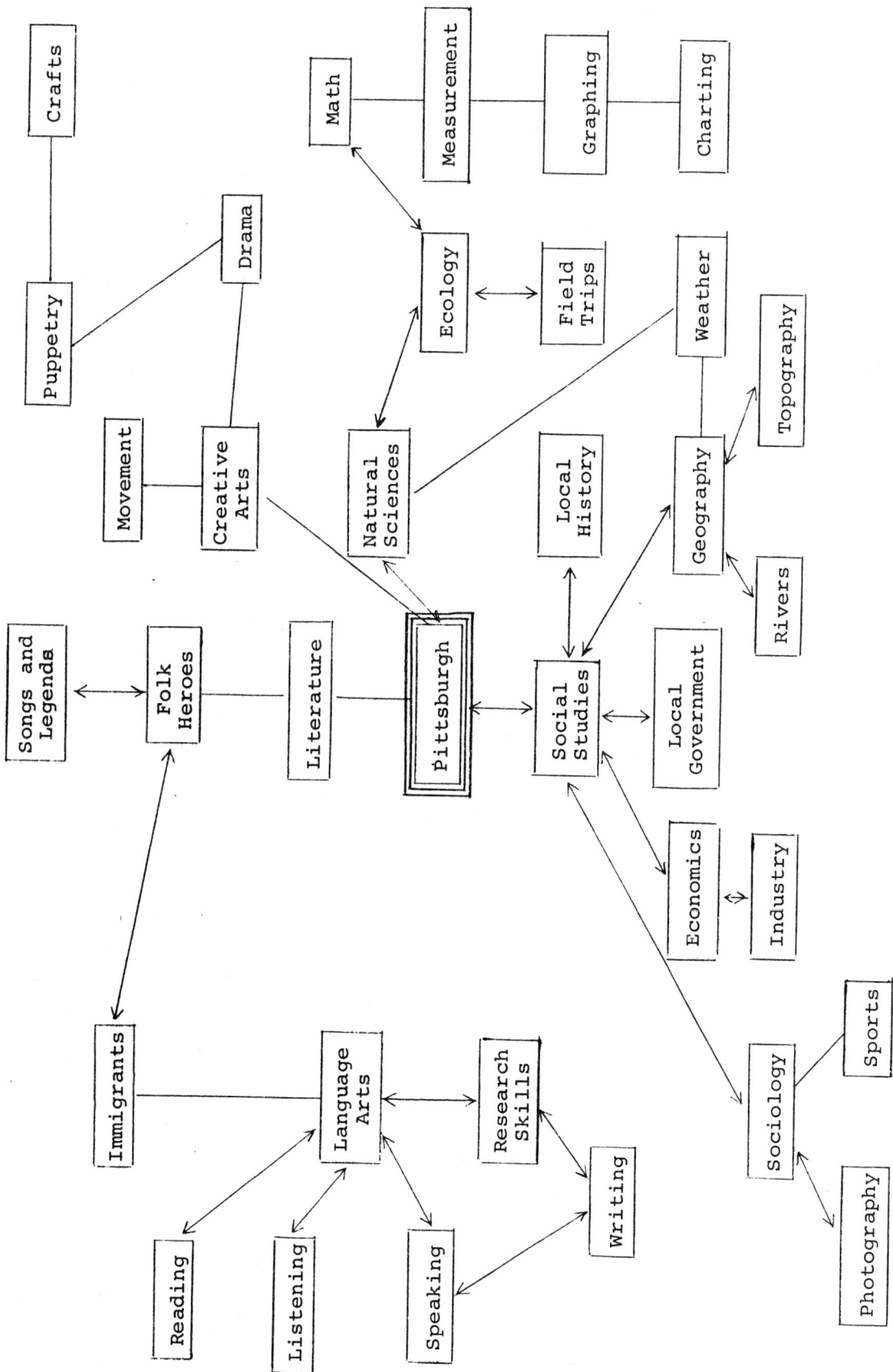

DIAGRAM III

Crafts

Puppetry — Drama

Math — Measurement — Graphing — Charting

Ecology ↔ Field Trips

Weather

Movement — Creative Arts

Natural Sciences

Local History

Geography ↔ Topography

Geography ↔ Rivers

Songs and Legends ↔ Folk Heroes

Literature

Pittsburgh

Social Studies ↔ Local Government

Economics ↔ Industry

Immigrants

Language Arts ↔ Research Skills

Reading

Listening

Speaking

Writing

Sociology ↔ Sports

Sociology ↔ Photography

55

CHAPTER 5

CREATING THE LEARNING ENVIRONMENT

What are the elements of an effective learning environment? The most basic requirement is flexibility. As long as teaching and learning remain human endeavors, the surroundings in which it takes place must be easily amenable to change, as the human needs change.

Regardless of the age or the design of the physical facility, certain criteria must be met in order for it to function effectively. These criteria apply to all schools -- urban, suburban, rural, rich or poor.

1.   Light, heat and sound: Lighting should be soft and pleasant. Temperatures should be moderate and easy to modify. Acoustical treatment enhances communication.

2.   Display space: Many new buildings sacrifice bulletin board areas for ceiling-to-floor windows, brick interior walls and other architectural features. Display is a very important mode of communication. It is an effective way of sharing ideas and feelings. It can motivate and reinforce learning and establish acceptable standards of work. Through displaying children's work, attractively mounted, the adults "tell" them that their products are valued.

3.   Storage: "A place for everything and everything in its place." Adequate and convenient storage space is especially important in the development of an informal classroom, with its emphasis of independent activity. Children need to have easy access to materials and resources. Cleaning up is greatly simplified by clearly labeled shelves and cupboards.

The teacher needs storage space for files, records, office supplies and his personal belongings. Arrangement for storage of supplies which will be rotated periodically throughout the school year needs to be made. Adequate space for coats and boots will reduce clutter and messiness. An environment which is tidy and orderly invites caring for it.

4. Safety: The environment should be arranged in ways which permit rapid evacuation of children in emergencies. The boundaries, both inside and out, should be clearly defined, with ground rules concerning the activities which take place. In the United States, teachers are responsible for all their children and, therefore, should know where they are. In some schools in England, there is a more casual attitude about this and children are seen frequently working out of sight and hearing of any adult. Safety considerations vary in different regions of our country.

5. Furnishings: Multi-purpose, portable furniture is highly desirable, so that the environment can be altered to match the changing needs of the children. It should be sturdy, easy to clean and comfortable. Carpeting and pillows add an inviting and informal quality to the environment. Teachers can add interesting furnishings to create an attractive setting.

6. Space: There must be provision for small group, large group and individual activity. Privacy may be achieved by moving portable chalk boards, storage cabinets, etc. to partition a small area. Another consideration is the separation of noisy from quiet activities. With the absence of a desk for every child, individual storage places are needed for each child.

A definition of the learning environment may be expanded to include the people -- the human element -- custodial staff, cafeteria workers, parent volunteers, teachers, student teachers, aides and administrators, all influencing the atmosphere in which the lives of children are being shaped.

New Open Space Buildings

Exciting, bold design in school buildings can be observed in rural, suburban and urban areas throughout the country. The current architectural trend is toward new open-plan buildings. The impetus for change came from the growing dissatisfaction with the inflexibility and sterility of the old "egg-crate" design of school buildings. Educators and curriculum developers are responsible for creating pressure for new physical facilities. The spread of non-gradedness and team teaching was hindered by conventional settings.

Planning for a new building, at best, should be the combined effort of the architects, delegates of many levels of school personnel and parent representatives. The planning process is complex and difficult. School people, parents and architects have to work hard at communicating with each other. Feasibility and cost have to be considered as important factors in planning.

The planning committee is charged with articulating the educational priorities of the community which then suggest particular building features. In this way, the new building will serve the educational program rather than the other way around.

Assuming the responsibility for planning represents a long-range commitment on the part of the participants. Plans may evolve over a period of several years. This planning time may also be utilized for in-service programs designed to prepare the staff to work in an open-space environment.

Land purchase and building sites will vary widely from community to community. Taxpayers, in some areas, are reluctant to approve large expenditures for buildings which will be used for only part of the day and part of the year.

Other more progressive communities are planning for the year-round school concept. New schools are being built in community parks which permit educational and recreational activities to be integrated throughout the year. Still other communities are combining the school with the delivery of social and health services.

The Materials Resource Center or the media library is usually located in the center of the building, giving easy access to everyone. This arrangement lends support to school-wide sharing of materials and equipment so that individual possessiveness is discouraged and duplication is diminished.

The Walnut Hills Elementary School of the Cherry Creek School District in Colorado demonstrates the central position of the library. They also managed to save a considerable amount of money by cataloging only very expensive or irreplaceable books. The library is in constant use, by individual children and by teachers with groups of children. Some books disappear, but the cost is minimal when compared to the cost of cataloging, shelving and checking systems.

No single model or design of a school building will match everyone's philosophy or educational goals. Buildings will be modified once they are occupied in order to adapt to evolving programs.

In the past 25 years, new school construction has tended toward larger and larger buildings. Part of the reason for this is economic; part has come from the consolidation of small school districts.

Decisions about school building come primarily from school board members and legislators, many of whom view the "business of education" with a business-and-industry mentality which em-phasizes efficiency and productivity. The dominant American value, "Bigger is better" is expressed in the proliferation of new elementary schools built for 1,000 small children.

As long as school is viewed as a "factory," it will in-herit all of the evils of the assembly line -- depersonalization, monotony, and crowding. Industry is now recognizing that life on the assembly line is sterile, dull and frustrating leading toward absenteeism, emotional problems and faulty products. Should not the school examine its internal life?

The writers visited many primary schools in England. Some

were new and purpose-built with open spaces and charming court-
yards. Some were old and ugly, cramped and crowded -- but few
housed more than 400 children. Again and again, we were struck
with the quality of life in these buildings, which we believe
is a direct consequence of the number of children. The head of
a small school can really know all the teachers, all the children, all the parents, and they can know him and each other.

Historically, most school districts organized their
schools with first grade to eighth grade in one building and
ninth through twelfth in another. This was changed to 1-6, 7-9,
10-12, or elementary, junior high and senior high school. More
recently, there is a trend toward the Middle School, with K-5,
6-8, or 6-9 and senior high school.

> As one looks at present organizational approaches to
> education in the United States, it is obvious that a
> great deal of variety exists from one district to
> another. Schooling may begin at two or at five or
> even at six or seven years. School-leaving ages
> vary and the graded system is downright confusing -
> often seeming to be based on what buildings of what
> sizes happened in the past to have been built in the
> school system. Thus we have an enormous spectrum of
> plans: K-3-3-6, N-K-3-3-2-4, K-6-6, K-8-4, and so
> on. Paradoxically, the extent to which the numerical
> variety is permeated by bureaucracies is essentially
> similar...many attempts to create "open" or more
> relevant schools have foundered on bureaucratic
> shoals and reefs (Shane, 1973).

Perhaps the next logical reorganizational step should be a
separate unit for the primary children, K-3. These are the
crucial years in the child's school life -- the time when not
only are basic skills acquired, but attitudes toward self,
toward school and toward learning are developed. This may be
an excellent way of providing smaller administrative units and
more human learning environments for both children and school
personnel.

New Ways in Old Buildings

Many school people have been heard to say, "I would like
to adopt the informal approach to education, but I work in an

old building which doesn't permit me to do it." Such a statement may be made out of ignorance, or it may be an excuse for maintaining the status quo.

On the other hand, there are school districts where dramatic changes in the educational program have been achieved in existing facilities. It was pointed out in Chapter III that movement toward the informal classroom was most likely to occur where nongradedness and team teaching had already been put into practice. Once there is philosophical agreement among the staff, it is possible to re-examine the utilization of space and other resources. Sometimes, a beginning can be made by one team in a school who come to a common definition of goals and set an example for the rest of the faculty. The principal must be supportive of change, willing to allow it to take place over time, and able to protect the team from opposition and ostracism by other faculty.

Such a team could begin by sharing children, by allowing children to flow back and forth between classrooms, sharing apparatus and equipment, and by developing complementary learning centers. This approach diminishes duplications and helps teachers move away from the possessive "mother-hen" attitude about "my children" which characterizes so many teachers of young children. It also reduces the loneliness of being the sole adult in charge and provides collaboration and partnership.

Cooperating teachers should be located in classrooms physically close to each other to facilitate sharing of materials, to facilitate good traffic patterns, and to avoid the pitfall of disturbing the rest of the school.

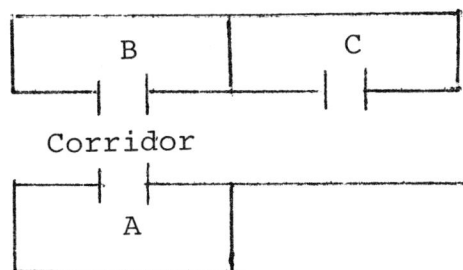

Classroom A can be designated as the construction and creative arts area, where noisy building activities can take place without disturbing others. Classroom B can house math, science and social studies and C can become the reading and language arts base.

This is an economical way of trying out a cooperative informal approach, without making any structural changes or investing a large amount of money. If it is successful, it may then persuade others to consider new buildings which are built especially for this approach, or to consider making physical alterations of existing buildings.

Simple modifications, such as removing doors from connecting classrooms, should be made before greater changes are undertaken. Storage areas which serve no real function and large cloakrooms can be converted into learning areas. A balcony with a ladder can serve as a library and reading area.

As a result of the evacuation of children from the cities in England during World War II, all kinds of improvisation by the teachers had to be made, converting quonset huts and bomb shelters into schools. Teachers in England have had more time to solve some of these problems and there is much we can learn from them in finding new ways in old buildings.

Some school districts in the United States have demonstrated creative uses of unconventional buildings like warehouses, lofts and storefronts. These ventures are usually the product of a collaborative effort by school personnel and parents who are searching for alternatives within the public school framework.

Planning new ways in old buildings, it must be emphasized, should be as unhurried as possible and should grow out of the defined objectives of the faculty. There should be adequate preplanning by the educators before the architects are consulted. A feasibility study and cost estimates are helpful in the early planning stages.

Grouping for Instruction

During in-service workshops for teachers, a common question is "How do we begin grouping for instruction in an informal classroom?" The established practice of assigning the children to three groups may be one way to begin.

Grouping children for direct instruction in an informal classroom is a flexible and continuous process. It is based on teacher observation of each child's performance. The groups are fluid and may change from day to day. Direct instruction of a particular concept may be introduced by the teacher and followed up by peer teaching as one or two children achieve mastery.

The teacher is in a position to identify the child who needs more practice in a skill, and to provide it quickly, through re-grouping, before the child experiences any sense of failure. The teacher, through observation, can direct a child to a learning center in order to provide him with specific material designed to remedy his deficit. Remedial or corrective activity need not be limited to only one learning center but may occur in several. For example, the child who drops word endings while working in the language arts center can be given help in this in the math or music area.

Adequate diagnosis by the teacher, shared with the student, is essential. Individual or small group instruction must be designed to meet the needs of the children. Flexible grouping based on skill development, interest areas, outgrowth of projects, etc., provide the teacher with the "who". The "how" depends on his creativity and his competencies.

The process of grouping during the first several weeks takes on a different focus. This is the time when careful initial observation of particular interests, skill acquisition and socialization can be observed. The data collected during these initial weeks are a springboard for determining the early grouping and the development of theses which are of particular interest to the child.

Initially, the teacher groups the children arbitrarily, and randomly assigns them to learning centers. After the first several weeks of careful observation, assessment and documentation, the teacher is then able to form groups on a more sophisticated basis, avoiding labels, and grouping which is based on actual performance levels.

Learning Centers

What is the difference between learning centers and inter-est areas? In conventional classrooms, the interest areas were developed as a way of grouping or displaying instructional material. The children could go to an interest area, such as a classroom library, and take material back to their desks. The learning center, in contrast, is an active and functional place in the classroom, a place where the learning occurs.

Some teachers, in conventional classrooms, provide the children with supplementary activities to be done after they finish their assigned work. Frequently, these are dittoed work sheets which penalize the more able learner and repetitive work rather than stretch him or allow him to follow his interests.

Just as there is no single model of an informal classroom, there is no single model of a learning center. Each will develop and grow out of the specific needs and preferences of a teacher and the children. There are, however, some basic elements to be considered.

An effective learning center gives the children opportuni-ty to test, to see, to measure, to prove, to find out, to record, to do, to took at, to experience things for themselves. The center should be monitored by the teacher to make sure that it meets the needs of the children. Directions and guidelines for the use of each learning center need to be clearly established so that children can function comfortably on their own. It may be useful for the teacher to demonstrate the use of materials, in order to guarantee safety and to maximize learning.

The learning center is designed to guide the child into problem-solving and exploratory activity. It should be attrac-tively arranged and inviting. It may consist of a work surface, shelves and other storage space, appropriate tools and materials, wall charts, and task cards.

The teacher must determine how many learning centers are desirable in terms of available space, and how many children may be accommodated in each center. It is important that each center is generating similar levels of interest so that all the children do not gravitate to one center.

As the teacher looks at the classroom space in planning for learning centers, he will take into account the flow of traffic, proximity to other learning activities, and accessibility of electrical outlets, water and other necessities. One area may be carpeted to communicate the idea that quiet activities are encouraged there.

Each center should be stocked with activities at many levels or difficulty so that every child may encounter success. Levels of difficulty can be indicated by a color-coding system. A wall chart can provide an illustrated list of vocabulary relevant to the center to assist the child in independent writing activities.

Learning centers need not only be found in the self-contained classroom or pod. Many effective learning centers in England and the United States are found in hallways, cloakrooms and foyers, or in areas which are not considered instructional space. In geographic locations where the climate permits, outdoor court yards are excellent areas for learning centers to be established -- for arts and crafts, woodworking, gardening and informal music.

The teacher's role changes as the environment changes. With the development of learning centers and the increasing independence of the children, the teacher is relieved of his station at the front of the room and is free to move around, offering suggestions, answering questions, formulating other questions, reinforcing, enjoying and noting children's problems and possible solutions.

Learning Materials

For some inexperienced practitioners, learning centers have become synonymous with task cards. Task cards are just one component of an effective learning center. They play an important role in the center by suggesting how the other materials may be used. They may also suggest starting points, provide motivation, and structure activity.

Learning materials are introduced to the children by a responsible adult who will explain and demonstrate how they are to be used. This applies to games, puzzles and apparatus which the task cards indicate are to be utilized. The task cards enable the child to work independently, without direct supervision by the teacher. Each new piece of learning material needs to have a place where it is stored so that clean-up is facilitated. Materials should be rotated periodically so that high interest is maintained.

Creating effective task cards is not easy. It involves more than reproducing textbook exercises on individual cards. The following attributes should be kept in mind in developing them:

1. They should be clear and simple and within the reading capabilities of the children.
2. They should be made of durable material and may be color-coded according to level of difficulty or to coordinate with color-coded material in other content areas.
3. They should direct the child into "doing something," i.e. answering a question, solving a problem, or performing an experiment.
4. They may suggest how to begin, where to look, what to use.
5. They should suggest methods of verifying results.
6. They should suggest alternative ways of communicating the findings -- writing, telling, painting, etc.

These attributes of teacher-made task cards can also be used in evaluating commercially produced materials.

Children learn through play. Therefore, games and puzzles in each learning center will offer many educational opportunities and add to the appeal of the center. Although the uninformed observer may view this kind of activity as frivolous "fooling around," the use of well-chosen sturdy games can fulfill many instructional objectives. An example of a simple game the teacher can make follows: Using the inside of the bottom part of a hosiery box, divide it into six sections with a marker or crayon. Find 6 pairs of pictures - 3 pairs beginning with M and 3 pairs beginning with B.

Mm   Bb

Mount the duplicate pictures on cardboard, put them in the box, close it with a rubber band. Decorate the box and color-code it. (Language Arts and Level of Difficulty).

For more mature children, the upper and lower case letters may be added at the top of the box and the words printed on the back of the picture cards. The children may either match the pictures or the letters.

Material can be either commercially produced or teacher-made. Some ideas for making games, puzzles and teaching devices are:

Games Formats

1. Dice and board games
2. Spinner and board games
3. Variations of Dominoes
4. Card games
5. Bingo variations
6. Lotto variations
7. Battery-operated games
8. Floor games - hopscotch, twister
9. Riddles
10. Variations of Twenty Questions
11. Timer games (like Spill 'n' Spell)

Puzzle Formats

1. Jig-saw
2. Crossword
3. Follow the dots
4. Scrambled words and scrambled sentences
5. Anagram
6. Scrabble

Teaching Devices

1. Lacing and matching charts
2. Pocket charts which invite participation
3. Shoe Box units which contain
   Dioramas
   Feeling Box
   Peep-hole
   Word file
   Science experiments
   Math experiences
4. Hosiery Boxes which contain
   Matching games
   Sorting
   Classifying
5. Salt and Oatmeal boxes which can be made into
   Containers for games
   Puppets
6. Word Wheels
7. Mobiles
8. Bulletin boards which invite participation
9. Kinesthetic games - box lid or tray filled with salt or sand for writing, printing, drawing, Magic slates
10. Graph paper
    Battle ship
    Travel games

Materials Resource Centers

The conventional locked library is being replaced in many schools by the concept of a central Materials Resource Center which is a functional part of the child's learning experience. It may be stocked over a period of years, to house media other than reference books, i.e. cassettes, films, film strips, transparencies, listening posts and other non-print resources.

It is used by teachers as well as all the children. In some schools, only the older children are permitted to use the Materials Resource Center. This is an unfortunate practice. Young children can learn to take care of materials and older children can help them.

Carrels provide places for quiet, independent research or study. The Materials Resource Center should be attractive and comfortable. The organization and accessibility of materials is as important in the Resource Center as in the classroom or pod. There should be ample space for aides and volunteers to prepare materials.

In new buildings, its location for maximum use should be considered. The school district may want to consider the possibility of making the center available for use by the entire community in the evening, or weekends and during vacations.

Beyond the School Building

On a pleasant day in the Spring or Fall, it is a common thing to see a class taking a walk to look for and collect signs of the changing seasons. Many schools permit a one-day field trip to a museum or other place of interest near the end of the school year. More attention, in recent years, is being given to finding ways of using the larger community as the classroom. Planned field trips are becoming more of an integral part of the on-going curriculum rather than a once-a-year happening. The goals and objectives of a field excursion should be clearly defined by the teacher and the children and shared with parents and administrators. As a learning experience, the field trip can be a powerful motivator. Children learn to take notes, to observe and to record their impressions in a variety of ways, by writing or painting, or through a photographic essay.

For example, as children become aware of the environment and problems of ecology, the neighborhood of the school can provide many learning experiences. They may choose to investigate any of the following social issues: garbage collection and disposal, safe play areas, sewage and sanitation, traffic and noise.

Study of this kind may be expanded to include comparison of local problems with national patterns. Documentary programs on TV, recommended by the teacher and viewed by the children in the evening, can provide additional information.

In their exploration of the neighborhood, children acquire research skills which will be of value to them. Change in our secondary schools is exemplified by greater use of the community for learning and the creation of "schools without walls." Early acquisition of investigative skills reinforces this trend.

CHAPTER 6

KEEPING TRACK

The Use of Standardized Tests

Evaluation and measurement activities have a legitimate and valuable place in education. We recognize the need for the systematic collection of data, but we wonder if educators in the United States are: 1) over-committed to testing programs, 2) using instruments which are appropriate for their objectives, 3) mis-using test results for tracking purposes.

Some educators in England and the United States are rethinking the whole issue. Standardized tests are based on national norms. There are standardized IQ tests, standardized achievement tests and standardized diagnostic tests. Generally, they have been predictive of performance in conventional classrooms using a traditional approach of teaching the text. Standardized tests are accompanied by many biases which do not take into consideration the individual child--his experiences, cultural and dialect differences and his emotional maturity.

Just as educators are exploring different ways of looking at children, test developers and other concerned people are re-examining tests, test procedures and their ultimate use. With new curricula being designed and the strategies of the informal classroom being implemented, there is growing, parallel need for improved methods of evaluation. Efforts in this direction are under way at the Education Testing Service, (ETS, 1973), CEMREL, (CEMREL, 1973), and the Intermediate Unit #22, Doylestown, Pennsylvania, (RISE, 1973), to name a few.

Because of funding requirements, it is usually the newest and, therefore, the most vulnerable programs which are subjected to the closest scrutiny. The children in conventional programs in most school systems are usually measured by standardized achievement tests and the programs continue regardless of the test results. The children in newer, promising approaches to learning are usually subjected to the same standardized tests, even if they do not match the program objectives, and if their test results are poor, the approach is discontinued.

Achievement tests provide a description of accomplishment. Diagnostic tests give information about strengths and weaknesses in the child. Neither offers direction to the teacher in how to compensate for the deficiencies which are identified. Parents are frequently informed of test results but, like the teacher, have little or no idea of what to do about them.

Test results can be misleading if a total score is utilized which masks individual sub-scores. For example, two children may have identical total scores, but each may have sub-scores which are very different from each other.

Another practice which may be damaging to the educational endeavor, is the use of test scores to rank children in a class or a school, or to rank schools in a particular district. Stereotypes are formed, expectations are shaped, and the self-fulfilling prophecy is set in motion. Some teachers use test scores to justify their request for transfer to what they perceive to be a better school. New teachers are typically given the children with the lowest scores and the high scoring children are assigned to the experienced teacher. If parents want the school to rank and sort the children, then tests are efficient instruments in carrying out this goal. If, on the other hand, their expectations are broader, then perhaps tests are given more importance than they deserve.

They may provide the teacher with a kernel of understanding, and, if used intelligently, can help in putting together a picture of the whole child. We would urge the avoidance of mass standardized testing because it generates high levels of anxiety in both the teacher and the children. A better practice would be for the teacher to use tests selectively with individual children about whom he needs additional information.

It should be added, parenthetically, that if achievement, as measured by standardized tests, is a defined objective of the school program, the curriculum, should reflect this and the children should receive instruction in how to take tests. In our test-oriented society, many decisions are based on test scores - entry into college, civil service, many positions in large corporations. Should the techniques of test-taking be taught - even in an informal setting? It is an issue not to be dismissed lightly.

Informal Evaluation by the Teacher

Most of us can accept individual physical differences among children. It is much more difficult to accept the wide range of intellectual, emotional and social differences that are present in every group of children. We do not expect that all seven-year olds will wear the same shoe size, but we tend to expect that all seven-year olds will reach the same level of achievement in a given period of time.

Any evaluation effort must be closely associated with both the behavioral and affective objectives which have been defined. Optimally, they should grow out of the process of defining the goals and should be known to the teacher and the children before the learning activities are begun. For example, if the goal is to find out whether plants need light in order to grow, it is a simple matter to determine if the child did indeed find out, and for the teacher to record this information.

The teacher needs to consider two kinds of record-keeping. He needs records for internal use within the classroom, which will provide feedback and guidance for the teacher. In addition, the teacher needs to gather information for sharing with school personnel and with parents. Evaluation in an informal, individualized setting must be carried out on an individualized basis, concentrating on the growth of each child, and avoiding comparison and ranking. Moving toward this kind of evaluation will require the re-education of teachers, principals, parents, and even of children, all of whom have been conditioned to make comparisons. It will take time until teachers develop enough confidence in their ability to evaluate the child's individual growth so that they can then persuade parents and others of the validity of such assessments.

The teacher must be convinced that informal evaluation of the individual child will be of value in several ways: 1) it provides information for the teacher which will indicate what materials and learning activities are needed; 2) it provides evidence of progress which can be shared with the children, other school personnel and parents; 3) it assists the teacher in organization and planning; 4) it provides the teacher with the opportunity to determine whether his behavioral and affective objectives have been met.

There are several strategies among which the teacher may choose, depending on his skills and sophistication. It may require some experimentation until the teacher discovers the most appropriate and the most comfortable arrangement.

1. <u>Anecdotal record</u> - This should be a running account of the growth of the individual child. For this kind of record to be effective, the teacher must have a focus and know the questions which need to be answered. It is of greater value to note that Johnny successfully completed Task A, B, and C than to record that "Johnny worked well today."

A file of 5x8 cards is a convenient device on which to record observations. It is easier to maintain than a notebook. The cards can be stored alphabetically for accessibility. From the anecdotal record, generalizations can be drawn for reporting to parents and others.

Some anecdotal records may be stored in a learning center and may contain information about the mastery of the skills related to that center. Other records may be kept centrally and would reflect each child's behavior in large group activities such as story time, music and movement. This is also an effective way for the teacher to check on his own interactions and to make sure that he is not overlooking any children.

Each entry should be dated. If a parent or principal makes an unscheduled visit, the teacher has concrete, up-to-date information about the child's performance. The anecdotal record can serve as an effective means of communication with aides and volunteers. An entry which says, "Michael needs more practice in counting," or "Sue is still having trouble finding main ideas in reading," gives specific direction in working with that child. Periodically, in the interest of good housekeeping, and to enable reporting to parents and others, the teacher will summarize the anecdotal entries and transfer them to a journal, and begin a fresh set of note cards. This may be done at the end of report periods and provides opportunity for systematic review of individual progress. It is also an expedient way of determining if stated goals have been reached.

If the teacher has clearly formulated questions about the child's performance, then anecdotal entries need not be time consuming. The use of file cards is one method of keeping anecdotal records which seems to be successful. Other methods may be employed as well. If a teacher writes about five children at the end of each day, he will be able to record the activities of 25 children per week.

2. <u>Individual pupil folders</u> - Folders made of sturdy material can be maintained in a file drawer. The folder may contain samples of the child's work--art, creative writing, math, etc. These are useful in conferences with children, parents and others. Children can share the responsibility for maintenance of the folders.

From time to time, the child and the teacher may go through his folder and decide what he may want to take home. Some samples should be retained in order to see progress across the entire year. If a child has written a lot of poetry in a given period, he may want to bind it into a book of verse.

3. <u>Analysis of activity</u> - The teacher, from time to time, steps back from the class in order to determine the quality of a child's interactions in a learning center. Is it superficial dabbling? Is he avoiding some activity? Is the child engaged in problem-solving? Are additional materials needed? Is he using time wisely?

The teacher uses the information he has gathered to improve and enhance the learning situation. The use of this particular strategy shifts the emphasis from blaming a child for his failure to "what can I do to help this child to learn?" "Are our instructional objectives clearly stated?"

4. Children's projects - The teacher can assess skill development in the application of concepts to projects originated by the children. A child's construction can be the demonstration of his competency in measurement. Language development can be evaluated through informal conversation, dictated stories, creative writing, dramatic play, puppetry, and children's diaries.

Although the finished product is valued, the teacher is most interested in the thinking processes that led to it. The teacher asks, "What did the child have to do in order to carry out this project?"

It is possible to gather a great deal of useful information about the child if the teacher is an active listener. Teachers often talk too much and tend not to listen enough. Listening to children's conversations at play, in the science center, at the clay table can provide the teacher with clues to the child's interests, his worries, his fantasies as well as his understanding and his skills.

How often does the teacher engage a child in informal conversation? Again, many teachers are too busy explaining and giving directions to initiate a dialogue. Conversations between teacher and child can be helpful in the evaluation process and can help the child begin to learn how to evaluate himself.

Ash and Rapaport (1960) state, "Perhaps one of the most important contributions we can make to children's all-round development is in helping them to evaluate their work and behavior ...It is significant that where children are used to evaluating their work (in discussion) they accept criticism of individual work in an objective and positive way." (p. 125-127).

Discussion can be a useful vehicle for both the teacher and the children for evaluating their work. The teacher is responsible for creating and maintaining a positive climate in which the discussion takes place, and for framing questions which will stimulate thinking and require more precise and definitive language use on the part of the children.

"In a class of children aged eight to ten years some of the questions that were discussed about their original poems were:

1. Do you think the poem really matters to the person who wrote it?

2. Are there any words that help the meaning of the poem? Do they make you hear or see or feel more strongly?

3. How well does the rhythm match what the poem is about?"

(Ash and Rapaport, 1960, p. 127).

The child who learns how to evaluate himself objectively gains skills which he can use in school and throughout his adult life.

Record Keeping

In a conventional classroom, the task of keeping records is often a formidable one--viewed by many teachers as tedious bureaucratic clerical busy work. And, perhaps, sometimes it is. The responsibility for keeping track of individual and group progress in an informal classroom can be even more formidable and deserves some careful thought.

The teacher first needs to decide what to record. It is literally impossible to monitor all the activities which occur in a classroom, especially in an informal setting where the children are more likely to be engaged in a variety of individual tasks. At the beginning of the school year, as the teacher is getting to know the children, his efforts will be primarily concerned with gathering information about the children's experiences, interests and level of language.

This information, recorded anecdotally, provides the teacher with knowledge of the ability and achievement range of the class, and assists in formulating the instructional and affective objectives of his program. Deciding what to record is then based on those objectives.

Through this gathering of information, the teacher is

made sharply aware of the diversity in the children, and must plan accordingly. Meeting the individual needs of children may be accomplished through either whole class, individual or small group activity. In well-planned whole class or small group instruction, children may have learning experiences at many levels. For example, during the process of a group-dictated story, some children may simply gain experience in listening, others may listen and contribute, and still others may listen, contribute and read some of the words. The teacher may want to construct a simple checklist on which to record the level of each child's performance. In order to create such a checklist, the teacher needs a clear definition of the skills he expects the children to acquire. Some teachers, in the beginning, may need help in finding existing checklists from which he may draw items which are appropriate for his unique population. Many checklists or inventories have been published for the preschool, primary or intermediate level.

There are checklists and inventories which are designed to assist the teacher in dealing with skills, interests and social development. A skill checklist can be found in DeBoer and Dollmann's *The Teaching of Reading*, (1970) which presents a condensation of an informal reading inventory used at The University of Miami Reading Clinic. Another skill checklist is presented in Harris and Smith's *Reading Instruction Through Diagnostic Teaching*, (1972). It features differentiated levels of proficiency. The book also presents a checklist which the child uses to document what he enjoys doing in his leisure time. This assists the teacher in gaining insights into individual children's interests. Simple skill checklists for the beginning reader may be found in *Teaching Them to Read*, (Durkin, 1970).

There are similarities between checklists and informal inventories. Both tools provide the teacher with an organized and systematic way of gathering information. Silvaroli (1973) has developed a *Classroom Reading Inventory* which features the measurement of skill development. A sample interest inventory is presented in Harris and Smith's book which was cited earlier.

In conducting in-service workshops, we frequently encounter initial resistance from some teachers around developing record-keeping devices. However, many teachers have reported to us that the very process of developing checklists has provided them with two unanticipated benefits:

1. A more concrete, detailed profile of each individual child and his needs.
2. A sharper definition of the specific skills which are embedded in the curriculum.

Teachers have found that, after several months, they no longer need to rely as heavily on the checklists because they had internalized the skills, and know the children better.

The teacher will also want to keep track of the social-emotional or affective growth of the children. The very climate of the informal classroom, which encourages affective development, dictates a need to monitor and record this growth. This is, in some ways, a more difficult task because of its subjective nature, but it is not impossible. Again, a clear definition of goals will minimize the subjectivity.

A number of checklists have been developed which deal with the child's social and emotional growth and development. The reader is directed to *Language Skills in Elementary Education*, (Anderson, 1964) for an example.

Another checklist may be found in *Educational Horizons* (King-Stoops, Winter 1972-73). Alternative schemes for record keeping are described in *Change for Children*, (Kaplan et al, 1973).

The primary purpose of much of this record-keeping is internal, that is, providing the teacher with continuous information about what is going on in the classroom or pod so that the program may be modified accordingly. From time to time, the teacher may summarize the information in order to communicate with other school personnel and parents about the child's growth and development.

Time invested in selective and appropriate record keeping is time well spent. Although some teachers will view this kind of activity as an intrusion into teaching time, it will become apparent that the systematic and continuous collection of data will be of great value in the planning for effective teaching. The greatest amount of time in the record-keeping process will be spent in designing and setting up the system. Once it is established, it will consume little time and effort.

As stated earlier, it is important and valuable to help children learn how to evaluate themselves. One of the effective ways of doing this is to enlist the child in the record-keeping process. The teacher can begin, through discussion with the children, to decide cooperatively what the children feel is important to record. They need to answer the following questions: What do I want to record? What can I record? How will it help me? and How long will it take?

Older children will be able to use more sophisticated techniques of record-keeping. Some children find keeping a diary or a journal a frustrating chore and for others it is an exciting and satisfying experience. The teacher can help match the recording system to the child so that it does not generate more than manageable stress. Record-keeping is a developmental process and the teacher who is well-grounded in child development theory can adapt the record-keeping task to the child's developmental level.

Record-keeping, initially, provides the teacher with information about each child--his strengths and his needs. This helps in planning instructional activities and in individualizing the learning process. Ultimately, as the child is drawn into the process of self-evaluation, he will not only develop an understanding of himself as a learner in the moment at hand, but he will also grow toward increased self-awareness and responsibility.

Frequently, when new programs or approaches are introduced in school, they are evaluated only by the academic achievement of the children. This is only one dimension of a program. Sound evaluation is based on the stated objectives of the program. The use of conventional evaluation techniques is not appropriate in the informal classroom and will yield incomplete or distorted information.

Valuable information about children may be gathered in conferences with the school psychologist, the social worker, the counselor, and with specialist teachers. Parents and guardians can share their observations of their children's behavior and activity outside of the school which can illuminate and deepen the teacher's understanding.

The more imaginative teacher will find ways of using existing materials and hardware for keeping track of children's progress. For example, in one classroom, the teacher recorded the spelling words for each lesson on Language Master cards. The test card for a lesson was placed in an envelope and numbered. When a child felt he was ready, he would go to the Language Master, put on the headset and test himself by writing the dictated words. This could be checked later by the teacher or aide. Using this technique permits each child to progress at his own rate, ensures his successful performance, frees the teacher from the weekly testing chore, and provides the child with an opportunity to be responsible for this part of his learning. It may be used from year to year.

The use of videotape equipment is increasing in school settings. Once the camera has been absorbed by teachers and children as a natural part of the classroom, it can be employed to great advantage to provide children with honest and objective feedback about their performance and behavior. For example, a disruptive child can be helped to see the dramatic difference between his behavior and his classmates' and the effect he has on classroom activity. Used judiciously, the videotape can be an effective means of modifying undesirable behavior.

Other Alternatives

The suggestions about evaluation and record-keeping which have been presented are not intended to be all-inclusive and definitive. The teacher or administrator may use the illustrations as starting points from which to develop their own techniques and formats. The very process of developing checklists and scales is essential to the definition and clarification of the teaching/learning program. The task is never done. School personnel must be willing to view evaluation and record-keeping as an on-going activity, under continuous scrutiny, subject to revision, refinement and extension. Engagement in continued review of the total evaluation process should lead to a curriculum which is appropriate and which takes into account the dynamic society in which we live.

CHAPTER 7

COMMUNICATING WITH PARENTS AND THE COMMUNITY

The Report Card

The process, method and format of reporting children's progress to parents must be tailored to meet the needs of each particular program and community. Just as there is no single model for an effective informal classroom or learning center, there is no single model report card.

Rance (1972) states:

"The controversy over the most suitable type of report card to send to a child's parents has gone on so long that it is quite impossible to suggest a form which is even going to remotely satisfy every shade of opinion." (p. 40).

At the end of a report period, in every home, in every classroom in the United States, teachers, children and parents agonize over the assignment of grades.

"Grade them low in the first report period so they can show improvement."

"Give him an 'A' for effort--he tries so hard."

"I always grade on a curve."

"If you bring home an 'A' in math, I'll give you a dollar."

"The teacher picks on me--that's why I never get an 'A'."

"If I give out too many 'A's, my colleagues will think I'm too easy on the kids."

"Remember, children, I didn't give you these grades, you earned them."

"How do you expect to get into college with grades like these?"

"Why don't you bring home grades like your brother's?"

"When I was your age--"

"But the teacher never calls on me--"

How many parents' signatures on report cards have been forged by anxious children? How many teachers have struggled to be fair? How many children are crushed and defeated by low grades?

Our entire society is regulated by the grading system, from kindergarten through graduate school. With computerized information retrieval, grades can follow the student through his whole life--a frightening prospect. Conventional letter grades are totally inconsistent with the philosophy of informal education. As more schools move in this direction, parents and teachers will have to re-examine this issue. They will find no easy answers but they must think through the values which are embedded in traditional grading and make some choices and compromises.

The report card format which is formulated is not particularly important. It is in the process of developing a report card format that vital issues are confronted and examined. Deciding what to report leads directly back to the clear definition of the objectives of the program. Criteria for evaluating children's progress need to be developed as well, i.e. what constitutes an outstanding performance? What indicates a need for improvement?

To illustrate the process, it may be helpful to examine the experience of a new open space elementary school (K-8) in an urban setting which was committed to moving toward the informal approach to education. The writers were deeply involved in planning activities with the administrators and some faculty before the school was opened, and continued as consultants and in-service leaders when the school became operational.

During the first weeks of the school year, the principal requested assistance in designing a new report card. Because of the informal philosophy adopted by the school, it was felt

I
GROWTH IN FUNDAMENTAL SKILLS

A - Excellent progress
B - Good progress
C - Fair progress
D - Slow progress
E - Unsatisfactory Progress

	First	Second	Third	Fourth
LANGUAGE ARTS				
Reading				
Fourth Reader				
Fifth Reader				
Sixth Reader				
Language				
Spelling				
Writing				
Social Studies				
Arithmetic				
Science				
Music				
Art				
Physical Education				
Teacher: If a conference with the parent is desired, check here				
Parent: If a conference with the teacher is desired, check here				

	First	Second	Third	Fourth
Days absent...........................				
Times tardy...........................				

GROWTH IN SOCIAL SKILLS

Your child is rated
by _____ teachers.
A check (✓) indicates the rating.

	FIRST		SECOND		THIRD		FOURTH	
	Satisfactory	Needs Improvement	Satisfactory	Needs Improvement	Satisfactory	Needs Improvement	Satisfactory	Needs Improvement
SOCIAL HABITS								
Is courteous and kind								
Shows self-control								
Gets along well with others								
Respects the rights of others								
Respects the property of others								
Respects school regulations								
WORK HABITS								
Pays attention								
Follows directions								
Does work neatly								
Uses time and material wisely								
Accepts responsibility								
HEALTH AND SAFETY HABITS								
Keeps neat and clean								
Reflects good sleep and other health habits								
Follows Safety rules								

strongly that the traditional report card used by the school district was inappropriate.

In discussions with the teachers, it was found that there was great diversity of opinion about the use of letter grades, about what should be reported, about criteria for evaluation, the use of standardized achievement test scores, and about every other aspect of the evaluation of children's progress.

During the same period of time, the consultant was meeting with a committee of concerned parents. School administrators participated in both the teachers' meetings and the parents' meetings. The consultant acted as the communicator between the groups. The parents demonstrated as much diversity of opinion as the teachers. The separate meetings for teachers and parents allowed the two groups to thrash out some basic issues without encountering each other as shouting adversaries.

Some of the parents wanted the school to abandon the use of letter grades. Others were reluctant to do so. A frequently voiced complaint was the experience they had had in other schools where the teacher would tell them their child was progressing well and the report card grades were B's or C's. Then, at the end of the year, the parent was told that the child had failed and needed to repeat the year.

When each group had sufficiently ventilated its feelings and had come to see the need for compromises, they were brought together. The following format was agreed upon, with the clear understanding that it was not a final product and would be subject to further refinement and change. (See Forms II)

During the following summer, a group of teachers with the administrators and the consultant drew up a revision of the form. The changes reflect growth on the part of the teachers and a growing clarification of the program. During the school year, each pod team had developed performance check lists in each subject area to help the teacher keep track of progress and to send home with the report cards. The check lists, for the most part, were drawn from the skills which were presented in the Teachers' Manuals in Reading and Mathematics. The process of developing the check lists helped the teachers to have the skills the chil-

II
SOCIAL SKILLS

Respects the rights and Property of Others				
Respects School Regulations				
Fulfills Responsibilities				
Respects School Personnel				

WORK SKILLS

Works Independently				
Works well with others				
Follows directions				
Completes assignments				
Makes good use of time				
Uses materials effectively				

Social Studies Units	Science & Health Units			

Conference desired ☐

PARENT'S COMMENTS

Conference desired ☐

TEACHER'S COMMENTS

Pupil's Name

School   Level - Room

Principal   Date

EXPLANATION OF MARKING

Progress & Achievement
- O Outstanding
- S Satisfactory
- I Improving but not yet satisfactory
- N Needs improvement

Sub-Areas
- + Very Strong
- ☐ Expected peformance
- = Below expectancies

	Peri-ods	1	2	3	4
READING					
Comprehension (incl. Word Analysis Phonics)					
Independent Reading					
ARITHMETIC					
Understanding Processes					
Knowledge of Number Facts					
Problem Solving					
LANGUAGE					
Spelling Skills					
Language Skills					
Language Written Expression					

SUGGESTED GUIDELINES FOR USING THE NEW EAST HILLS PROGRESS REPORT CARD

These guidelines pertain specifically to reading

PUPIL PERFORMANCE

EVALUATION MAY BE - O, S, N

Above level

O - Student fulfills required assignments in an outstanding manner. May also do extra work for special credit.

S - Student fulfills required assignment in a satisfactory manner with average success.

N - Student does not fulfill required assignments in a satisfactory manner, poor quality of work and little motivation.

At level

O, S, N

O - Student fulfills required assignment responsibilities in an outstanding manner with outstanding success.

S - Student fulfills required assignment in a satisfactory manner with average success.

N - Student does not fulfill required assignment responsibilities in a satisfactory manner. Poor quality of work, little motivation.

One/Half Year Below Level

S, N, N-(red)

S - Student fulfills required assignment responsibilities in a satisfactory manner with average success.

N - Student does not fulfill required assignment responsibilities in a satisfactory manner. Poor quality of work.

(red) N - Student does not fulfill required assignment responsibilities. Quality of work very poor. Very little motivation. Pupil shows signs of failing.

One/Half Year to ONe Year Below Level

S, N, N-(red)

Same as one/half year below level (see above)

One Year or More Below Level

N, N-(red)

N - Student fulfills required assignment responsibilities with average, or below average success.

(red) N - Student does not fulfill required assignment responsibilities. Quality of work very poor. Very little motivation. Pupil shows sign of failing.

dren needed at their fingertips. The report cards, therefore, did not have to be as detailed. (See Form III)

The third form will be submitted to the entire faculty and the parents committee for consideration early next term. Undoubtedly, the process will continue over many years, providing a valuable vehicle for ongoing communication between teachers, administrators and parents about vital aspects of the education of children.

Conferences

A useful way to communicate with parents is the conference. Although frequently associated with a once a year scheduled opportunity for a dialogue, conferences may occur in a variety of times and settings:

1. Casual encounters in the doorway of the classroom when a parent brings a child to school in the morning

2. Conversations in the supermarket, church or civic meeting

3. Discussions at PTA meetings (the invitation usually states explicitly that the child's performance is not to be discussed--what else is there to talk about?)

4. Scheduled parent-teacher conferences

5. Scheduled parent-teacher-principal conference about a serious problem

6. Scheduled parent-teacher-child conference--the most desirable format because it reduces the child's anxiety which would come from knowing that his parents and his teacher are discussing him without his participation

In the conventional teacher-parent conference, there are elements that are useful to employ when the school shifts to a more informal program.

1. The teacher should be prepared with concrete information and samples of the child's work that he can share with the parents. A positive approach by the teacher stressing the child's strengths

Pupil's Name

EAST HILLS SCHOOL

School _____ Level - Room

Principal **Gertrude J. Wade** _____ Date _____

EXPLANATION OF MARKING

Progress & Achievement | Sub-Areas
O | Outstanding | + | Very Strong
S | Satisfactory | | Expected
I | Improving but not yet satisfactory | = | Below Expec- tancies
N | Needs Improvement | | Performance

	PERIODS	1	2	3	4
READING					
Comprehension					
Work Knowledge (Incl. Phonics)					
Independent Reading					
ARITHMETIC					
Understanding Processes					
Knowledge of Number fact					
Problem Solving					
LANGUAGE					
Spelling Skills					
Language Skills					
Language Written Expression					
MUSIC					
ART					

SOCIAL STUDIES					
Subject Matter					
Research Skills					
Reports					
Projects					
Group Work					
SCIENCE					
Subject Matter					
Research Skills					
Projects					
Group Work					
PHYSICAL ED & HEALTH					
Health					
Skills					
Sportsmanship					
Participation					
SOCIAL SKILLS					
Respects the rights and Property of others					
Respects School Personnel					
Respects School Regulations					
Fulfills Responsibilities					

WORK SKILLS

Works Independently				
Follows Directions				
Completes Assignments				
Makes Good Use of Time				
Uses Materials Effectively				

Social Studies Units

Science Units

TEACHER'S COMMENTS

Conference Desired-----

PARENT'S COMMENTS

Conference Desired-----

91

may put the parents at ease and encourage them to share their own observations and concerns about the child.

2. The teacher should respond with interest to what the parents relate about the child's activities at home. Positive comments encourage the parents to speak more freely and the teacher is better able to gauge the parents' expectations of the child and of the school.

3. The professional teacher will see the tremendous worth of scheduling conferences at a time when both parents can attend.

Conferences may take the form of telephone calls or informal notes sent by teachers and parents. It may be a wise precaution for teachers to ask a colleague to look over a written note to check for ambiguous language and to avoid possible misunderstanding. Note-writing, if frequent, and not always negative can enhance communication. Class newsletters or school newspapers are effective methods of providing a closer link between home and school.

It may be advantageous and time-saving to schedule meetings with small groups of parents whose children share common interests. A principal of a new open-space building in a suburban school district arranged to attend informal coffees with small groups of parents in their homes for the express purpose of answering questions before the new building opened.

A common practice has been for teachers to meet with all the parents early in the school year in order to explain and describe the program for the coming year. As schools move toward the informal approach, this kind of meeting may no longer be appropriate. If the interests of the children and the teacher are to contribute to the shaping of the curriculum, the teacher will no longer be able to predict precisely what learning activities will take place. Class meetings or pod meetings may assume a different focus in an informal school characterized by lively discussion and the exchange of ideas.

The School and the Community

A common problem encountered in planning school-community

meetings is the fact that the people who would benefit most from attending rarely do. The school administration then usually berates those who have come for the apathy of the absent. The teachers in most school districts are expected to attend all meetings.

What are the techniques which can be employed to ensure good attendance and active participation in parent-teacher meetings?

1. A presentation by the children (a play, a musical program, a puppet show, a science demonstration, etc.) is guaranteed to draw at least the parents and friends of the children in the production.

2. The children, in action, can also be presented through a slide show, movies, or videotape.

3. A show and/or sale of arts and crafts produced by children, parents and teachers will draw an audience and stimulate interest and activity in the arts.

4. One of the most popular activities is sometimes known as the Fun Fair. This usually includes a bake sale, a drawing for prizes, booths, games, a book fair, etc. The preparation for the Fair helps to develop cooperative relationships among teachers, parents, children and administrators.

5. Workshops for parents, providing opportunities for them to follow a condensed schedule representing their child's day in school, interacting with their child's learning materials and his environment, give parents a concrete idea of the life of the school.

6. An agenda, published in advance, will encourage greater participation. This may include a demonstration of new teaching materials and apparatus and explanations and descriptions of new teaching approaches.

7. At any parent-teacher meeting, everyone should be informed, in advance, that there will be time, over refreshments, for parents and teachers to enjoy informal conversation. In order to protect the privacy of the individual child and family, the teachers will have their appointment calendars with them in order to schedule individual conferences.

8. In a school which is contemplating a move toward the

open classroom, it would be helpful to invite as speakers or as a panel, teachers, administrators, parents and children from other open classrooms.

"...American parents are perfectly capable of understanding and accepting informal education if it is explained to them..." (Silberman, 1970, p. 320).

9.   Parents are likely to attend meetings which feature outside speakers--college and university professors, civic leaders, child specialists, popular authors, career guidance specialists, school board members and speakers on child-rearing practices, discipline, etc.

10. Parents will respond to invitations to participate and share their views on such issues as report card format, long-range educational goals for their children, the after-school use of the facilities for recreation and adult education.

11. An evening event which features recognition of parent volunteers who have contributed time, skill and energy for the improvement of the school life of the child encourages continued support of the school. For example, The Reading is FUNdamental program in Pittsburgh, Pennsylvania sponsored a banquet at which teachers, principals, supervisors and the parent volunteers were honored.

12. A special night should be set aside to pay tribute to those children who have served the school community, i.e. the safety patrol, the ecology club, the softball team, etc.

The suggestions presented in this chapter are intended merely as starting points for developing good school-community relations. Implementation of these ideas will diminish the defensiveness often displayed by school personnel, and will shift the parents and teachers from adversaries to partners.

CHAPTER 8

LOOKING AHEAD

There has been much valid criticism of teacher preparation in this country. A large proportion of undergraduate teacher education occurs in large impersonal universities and state colleges. Most of the students never see a child until their senior year, when it is too late to change direction if the student discovers that he really does not like teaching. The string of required methods courses, with no opportunity for practical application with children, hardly equips young people for the complexity of teaching in today's classrooms.

Students who enter teacher preparation programs are largely the products of conventional, teacher-directed elementary and secondary schools. Most education courses are presented using traditional lecture-recitations. How does a graduate of this kind of elementary-secondary-college education begin to know how to function in an informal classroom if he has never experienced any of the methodology? (Silberman, 1970). In many schools of education, recommendation for certification is achieved by the accumulation of credits through courses which may not even be related to each other.

If the teacher is the critical variable in developing and implementing the informal classroom approach, then the preparation of teachers, at both the pre- and in-service levels, must be examined and reformulated. In many parts of this country, colleges and universities are vigorously re-shaping their teacher preparation programs. In remote locations, where students do not have easy access to public schools, the use of films, videotape and simulation games provide vicarious experiences. The depersonalization which often characterizes the multiversity is being tempered by the reorganization of the traditional arrangement of one professor for one course. It is possible to assign a group of students to a faculty team who work together over a period of one or two years, thus developing deeper personal relationships. This also facilitates the gradual evolution of partnerships made up of college and public school personnel.

Some Elements of Preservice Education

Primary to the development of an effective teacher preparation program is the role and function of the faculty. It is their responsibility to come together to define the philosophy, competencies, implementation and evaluation of the program. These definitions should be shared with the college student as he begins the task of becoming a teacher.

No longer should Schools of Education be content to mass-produce candidates for teacher certification. Only outstanding potential teachers should be recommended for entry into the profession.

A personal, individualized course of study is essential to the development of the beginning teacher. Only if the college student experiences individualization in his own learning can he be able to individualize instruction when he begins to teach.

The role of the professor requires re-definition. No longer is it appropriate to pull a dog-eared yellow folder of lecture notes from the file and present its contents to a class of bored listeners. There is, of course, a time for lecturing, but it is no longer sufficient to accomplish the enormous task of preparing teachers by simply regurgitating the wisdom of the ages.

> "Professors, in addition to begin impartners of facts and knowledge, must question, probe, recommend, urge, insist, support and reinforce the student. They are no longer exclusively responsible for the student's learning but help the student in becoming responsible for his own learning. The student may be uncomfortable in this new context, but will begin to see the rewards of learning for its own sake." (Morgan and Taylor, 1972).

An effective program will gather a faculty with diverse specialization to enable the student to have a wide range of human resources upon which he can draw. It is imperative that the faculty assess its own strengths and weaknesses and either compensate for deficiencies or seek outside specialists to assure that the college student can maximize opportunities for growth.

Learning is an active process. A sound philosophy will have at its roots structured experiences and learning activities. Ample opportunities for the student to ask appropriate questions and seek answers through systematic, scholarly study, coupled with first hand experiences with children should be provided where possible. As students combine first-hand experiences in learning/teaching situations with their exploration of the professional literature, it will become obvious that cognitive and affective learning cannot be separated. This awareness is reinforced by college faculty who must reflect concern for more than the cognitive development of the young adult.

A faculty should plan cooperatively to determine the expected competencies of their students. They should consider the composition of their expected population, the college's geographic location, current research findings, resources upon which they can draw, the physical facilities, materials, time, etc.

A Possible Prototype

The early childhood and elementary teacher education program at Chatham College, cooperatively with Carnegie-Mellon University (CMU), in Pittsburgh, Pennsylvania, has been in the process for the last several years of redefining itself in order to meet the changing needs of today's college students and the teachers of tomorrow's school children. The Chatham-CMU program consists of a flexible, individualized sequence of courses, experiences and seminars on both campuses, in the CMU Children's School, and in a variety of public and private schools in the community. The faculty is committed to the proposition that the process of becoming a teacher is both developmental and continuous. The program does not offer a major in Education. Students are expected to complete the requirements of the program in addition to their liberal arts studies.

The teacher education program is dedicated to the preparation and development of teachers who:

- are generally healthy and wholesome people who have achieved a moderate degree of self-awareness and self-understanding;

- are generally well-educated and have acquired competencies and skills in content areas and in problem-solving;

- have made a serious commitment to the education and development of children;

- understand the nature of the learner and the learning situation and can plan, with children, programs of activities which will facilitate and enhance the learning process;

- understand and be able to interact effectively with the school community and the larger society.

It is the intent of the faculty to maintain a program which is individualized and personalized, so that each student may be enabled to develop and grow in his or her own unique directions. The program is sufficiently flexible to accommodate to the individual differences among the students. Opportunity is provided for the development of human relationships between students and faculty, through counseling, instructional and informal contacts.

The philosophy of the program has evolved around several assumptions:

- learning is an active process which occurs most effectively when the student shares the responsibility for his own learning;

- the theoretical bases of education can best be acquired and integrated through many and varied opportunities for the student to apply them to practical, first-hand experiences with children;

- the integration of subject matter competencies with teaching methodologies is a more effective approach to the preparation of teachers than the traditional teacher training curriculum which features separate methods courses for each content area.

The scope of the program may be estimated by the course titles required for the completion of the Early Childhood and

98

Elementary Education sequences: Seminar in Education, Communication Skills in Education, Expressive Arts in Education, Early Childhood Curriculum, Elementary School Curriculum, The Young Child, The Elementary School Child, Teaching in an Urban Setting, and Student Teaching. Each course carries with it a field experience component of a minimum of one-half day per week in a classroom situation. This arrangement provides each student with at least five terms of supervised practical experience before student teaching.

Selected readings augment and enrich the student's growth. Library research grows out of the student's need to "find out" rather than being arbitrary, mass reading assignments. Systematic and scholarly study is an important part of the program, but it is not accomplished in a set, prescribed order.

The primary concern of the program is to provide and to structure appropriate learning experiences for each student. These experiences include lectures, demonstrations, discussions, films, micro-teaching, videotaping, interactions with specialist consultants, tutoring small groups and whole class instruction, library research, written assignments, and mutual peer evaluation. Students are given opportunities to observe master teachers, to have experience in and engage in critical analysis of a variety of classrooms (programmed, informal, traditional, experimental, etc.), lesson and unit planning, including the preparation of performance objectives, use of audio-visual equipment and techniques, team teaching experiences and self-evaluation techniques.

Early and continued exposure of the student to children in public schools serves several purposes.

a) It provides the faculty with ample opportunity to observe and evaluate the student as he grows and develops in the process of becoming a teacher. Data may be accumulated, based on the student's performance with children and other school personnel, and in conferences with the student, which enable the faculty to counsel out of the program those students who are dubious candidates and who may be profitably redirected to other areas of study early in their college careers. These experiences also permit

the early identification of the talented
student who may then be given encouragement
and support in developing his own unique
teaching style.

b)   It provides guided opportunities for the
student to test his own commitment to the
profession, to measure his own seriousness
of purpose, and to decide, without loss of
dignity or artificial pressure, whether or
not he belongs in the classroom.

In this way, students who enter the sequence for question-
able or unexamined reasons, (because the teaching certificate is
something to "fall back on," because teaching is an obvious
career choice for a young woman, etc.) either screen themselves
out of the program or are assisted by the faculty to choose alternative courses of study.

Students are advised and encouraged to register for related elective courses in other departments which will enrich
their preparation for the profession. Such courses may include:
Developmental Psychology, Child Performance through Movement,
Approach to Creative Dramatics, Cognitive Processes, Tests and
Measurements, Principles of Child Development, Child Psycho-
pathology, Literature for Children, etc.

An initial experience for the preservice teacher is an
opportunity to examine his own learning processes. This is a
step in helping the student analyze how children learn. Skilled
instructors aid the student in rediscovering that he learns
best through first hand experience and meaningful involvement
with the task. Children also learn in this manner. Subsequent
college courses in which students engage in the study of childhood reinforce the necessity of careful assessment of the pre-
service teacher's own thinking/learning process.

The program supports and encourages students in the pur-
suit of knowledge and experience through carefully planned
courses of Independent Study. Some students will use this opportunity to explore some aspect of special education. For example,
one student, in an Independent Study of Art Therapy for blind
children found that she had a strong aptitude for this work. She
designed additional Independent Study courses, with faculty

guidance, which enabled her to continue this work with emotionally disturbed children and children with learning disabilities over the next year and a half. She is applying for admission to graduate study in Art Therapy.

Independent Study courses have been designed to include experiences in educational television, alternative schools, Montessori schools, and in experimental settings. With the adoption of a new curriculum in 1970, Chatham College also adopted a new calendar which provides a one-month Interim term in January. The Interim permits students to carry out Independent Study plans which are field-based teaching experiences in other parts of the U.S.A. and other countries. When students return to the campus from Interim teaching experiences, they share these with others in the Education program. The Interim provides students with a one-month block of time during which they may engage in in-depth intense experience and growth.

The Education Department was able to offer a course which provided a living and teaching experience for selected students in Pennsylvania's Appalachia. They lived in and experienced rural poverty which they documented with film and tape. The local non-graded elementary school provided them with full-time teaching experience.

In subsequent Interims, some students went to Appalachia while others were selected to spend the month in Infant and Junior Schools in Norwich, England, where they lived with English families and worked full-time in the schools. The location was chosen as a result of a three-week exploration of the schools of England, undertaken by the writers and supported, in part, by the Central Research Fund of Chatham College.

After two successful Interim programs in Norwich, England, where with their professors, they engaged in seminars and discussions at the Teachers' Centre, efforts were made to bring some of the Norwich educators to Chatham College. In the Spring of 1973, the Buhl Foundation presented Chatham with a grant which enabled seven Norwich educators to spend three weeks in the Greater Pittsburgh area. Their visit was supported by Carnegie-Mellon University, the Pittsburgh Public Schools, The Regional

Council for International Education, the Urban League of Pittsburgh, and the Pittsburgh Council on Public Education. (Morgan, Richman and Taylor, 1973)

Their activity included: formal and informal meetings with staff from the Pennsylvania Department of Education in Harrisburg, seminars at Chatham College and CMU, teacher workshops, two major one-day conferences, and visits to informal schools and special programs in the Pittsburgh area. (Norwich Teachers' Centre, 1973).

A daily log or journal serves multiple purposes but basically provides a means of individual communication between student, supervising teacher and college faculty. Student growth is obvious when in this documentation he moves from the exclusive use of "I" to focus on discussing children in the classrooms.

A folder for each student is maintained cooperatively by students and faculty. A cumulative folder is an excellent resource for maintaining information of an autobiographical and developmental nature. Records of academic courses, test data, field experiences, notes from interviews and conferences, examples of research, etc., all provide avenues for individualizing a student's program. Frequent conferences with students assist the faculty in evaluating previous experiences, current involvements, and future goals. Emerging young adults are complex. Students today are engaged in a wide range of personal responsibilities and life styles which must be taken into consideration as a personalized teacher preparation program is shaped. Counseling and advising are time consuming and difficult tasks but absolutely essential.

Although course descriptions are framed in terms of performance objectives, it should be noted that the program has goals which cannot easily be described behaviorally or measured objectively. These goals, no less important than the competencies specified in the course descriptions, may be thought of as process goals. These include the following less-than-tangible and hard-to-measure qualities.

The development, over time, and through guided experiences, research and study, of:

a) wholesome and consistent attitudes toward children;

b) self-understanding, self-awareness and a developing sense of identity;

c) increasing understanding of and respect for children and adults who are culturally different;

d) the understanding that knowledge is uncertain and relative, that there may be more than one "right" answer,

e) the belief that problem-solving techniques and skills are more valuable than the rote acquisition of facts which may be forgotten or become obsolete;

f) acceptance, in theory and practice, of the assumption that each child is unique, and that the chief role of the teacher is that of facilitator and leader;

g) the understanding that the child's social and emotional development is inextricably related to his intellectual and academic growth;

h) a philosophy of education, a commitment to a set of values, and a unique teaching style.

"The preservice program is in an urban community. It is a becoming project...Without the cooperation of the public schools...our field oriented program would not be becoming." (Morgan, 1971, p. 170).

The potential college student today is much more selective in choosing a college than he used to be. He is looking for individualization, personalization, and for programs which will involve him in the world around him. He recognizes that college should not be "preparation for life" but should be life itself.

Some Elements of Continuing Education for Teachers

There are several ingredients which are essential for effective in-service programs:

1. Teachers should be involved in the planning for all in-service activities. Their needs, as perceived by them, must be considered, rather than what the administration thinks will be "good" for them. A consultant from outside the school system may be helpful in performing an objective needs assessment.

2. The administration must be active participants, alongside the teacher. This will heighten colleagueship, but it

may take time for initial awkwardness to be replaced by trust and openness.

3. The isolated one-day workshop will have only a temporary effect on performance. On-going, continuous education throughout the year, coupled with continuing support, will reinforce positive change.

4. The leaders of in-service activities should have demonstrated the competencies and the skills necessary in helping teachers to grow. They may be in-house personnel or outside consultants from colleges and universities, but they must have first-hand understanding of the problems facing each teacher. They must possess, in addition to their field of specialization, skills in group dynamics and interpersonal relations which will help others to learn and grow.

5. The leaders should be acquainted with the socio-economic level, the culture and the politics of the community. They should also be informed about history and background that prompted the in-service program.

The first-year teacher needs special attention. He is expected at the age of 22 or so, to step into his classroom, decorate it, organize it and manage the learning activities of 30 or 35 children. He may be plunged into a pod where he must work out relationships with other teachers in the pod and adjust to larger numbers of children. Any reader who has been a teacher can readily recall his own first-year's traumas.

In looking ahead, the new teacher needs to have access to a resource person in the building who occupies a non-judgmental, non-threatening, neutral and supportive role. The beginning teacher sometimes finds that if he requests help from his principal, supervisor or colleague, he may be regarded as incompetent. Frequently, all he needs is someone who can give him confidence and help him to become aware of what he already knows.

A good professional library which includes current books and periodicals should be available to the faculty. Team teaching or cooperative teaching offers a natural opportunity for the induction of the new teacher. There are more opportunities for informal conversation, discussions and sharing of frustrations and common concerns. The beginning teacher who is struggling to master a very complicated job and who may also be adjusting to a new marriage or independent life in an apartment, also needs guidance in pursuing post-baccalaureate study for permanent certification.

In contrast, the successful teacher who demonstrated competence over a period of six or seven years may become restive and begin to search for new challenges to master. This is the teacher who needs to have his excitement rekindled. This may be done in a variety of ways. The astute administrator is able to identify these teachers. Some school districts have created the position of Peer Teacher, which frees the teacher from the confines of the classroom and allows him to be a resource to other teachers. Some teachers have found inspiration through membership in professional organizations which gives them prominence, visibility and opportunities for leadership at local, state and national levels. Many effective teachers leave the classroom to assume supervisory, counseling, or administrative posts. There should be ways of retaining good teachers of children while meeting the teacher's need to continue to grow. The experienced, successful teacher may become excited at the prospect of becoming a demonstration teacher, serving as a model for the preservice student and visitors from other schools.

Some Perplexing Questions

We do not have all the answers. We may not even know all the questions. While the open classroom approach offers much promise in the education of children, we are left with many questions to consider.

Will school districts in the United States permit the development of the curriculum to occur school by school?

Will the State Department of Education eventually abandon content area guidelines?

With curricula imposed from above, how can the informal classroom utilize the individual interests of children and the teachers?

As American families continue to become more

mobile, is there a need for a standard basic curriculum?

The autonomy of the Heads of informal English primary schools brings advantages and disadvantages to issues concerning educational leadership, curriculum development and balanced emphasis in content areas. Where the Head is competent and responsible, the school reflects his expertise. What happens when he is not? Is this an organizational pattern we want to emulate?

Would autonomous Heads or Principals lead to isolation from other schools, other resources, and create inbred, ingrown faculties? How does creative change occur in school districts where school boards are elected through our political system?

Is it presumptuous to assume that the informal approach is sufficiently flexible to meet all the needs of the children, the teachers, the parents? Will it take time and in-service education to prepare teachers and administrators in the implementation of change? How do the educational leaders persuade the entrenched traditional teacher to consider the possibility of new approachers? Why has informal education encountered so much resistance in the secondary school?

Instant success is a typically American expectation. Are we able to permit a new educational approach to develop and stabilize over a period of years before passing judgment on it?

The evaluation of informal programs poses a complex set of problems. Often, research efforts are mistakenly equated with evaluation activities. While research and evaluation have some common and overlapping purposes, each really has distinctly different objectives. Evaluation is intended for providing feedback about the operation of the program to the decision-makers. Research on the other hand, involves the gathering of new knowledge, or the systematic measurement of program effect in experimental designs with control groups. (Hemphill, 1969).

No doubt the reader can add to the list of questions which need to be examined as we continue to search for ways to improve our schools.

Beyond the Open Classroom: Toward Informal Education

In the past two decades, we have witnessed and participated in massive upheavals and major shifts in public education across the nation. With about 70 percent of the population now concentrated in urban and metropolitan centers, the impact of these changes is felt most strongly by the urban schools (Hummel and Nagle, 1973).

Drachler wrote in the 1977 Yearbook of the National Society for the Study of Education:

> "The decades following World War II were years of unrest and anxiety in education. It was the era of Sputnik with its stress on science and the "new" mathematics, phonics, and "why Johnny can't read." Then the social-educational issues followed: the Brown decision and the neighborhood school, equal educational opportunity and Serrano, and compensatory education accompanied by accountability, performance contracts, and vouchers. The books of the period reflected the ferment and often implied the approach of an apocalyptic age: The Transformation of The School, Slums and Suburbs, Death at an Early Age, How Children Fail, Crisis in the Classroom and De-Schooling Society. Schools everywhere were affected by an avalanche of criticism - but urban schools became the major target." (page 194)

The 1960's were marked by an outpouring of federal funds which supported more innovative and experimental programs than had ever previously existed in urban schools. There were demands or a higher quality in education which led to the Right to Read program, Head Start, Follow Through and many others. There was an increase in the number of minority teachers and administrators, cultural pluralism in the curriculum, bilingual education and competency-based teacher education.

Among the changes which occurred in the late 1960's was the growth and proliferation of alternative schools, both within and outside of public school systems. The "open classroom," a journalistic phrase, which was sometimes confused with open-plan buildings, became a rallying cry for those in the profession who were influenced by the writings of Featherstone, Silberman et al. and who, like the writers, were excited and encouraged by the increasing use of informal teaching methods in the public schools.

The passage of P.L. 94-142, the Education for All Handicapped Children's Act, the continuing struggle in our cities to achieve desegregation and integration, coupled with the recent taxpayer's revolt and the "Back to Basics" movement can only combine to make the tasks of public education in the 1980's more complex and more difficult than ever before.

The informal approach to education, although it seems to have fallen momentarily out of fashion, continues to offer hope in the never-ending quest for a more effective, more humane way of life in our public school classrooms. There is ample room within the informal approach for individual school districts to develop their own unique style based on the particular characteristics, needs, desires, and dreams of their constituencies - the parents, the teachers, the school personnel, and the children.

REFERENCES

Anderson, Paul S., *Language Skills in Elementary Education.* New York: Macmillan, 1964.

Ash, B. and Rapaport, B., *Skills in the Junior School.* London: Methuen and Co. Ltd., 1960.

Banham, Katherine M. Individual Record Checklist. Maturity Level for School Entrance and Reading Readiness. Educational Test Bureau. Division of American Guidance Service, 720 Washington Ave. S. E., Minneapolis, Minnesota.

Brown, Mary and Precious, Norman, *The Integrated Day in the Primary School.* New York: Agathon Press, 1969.

Bruner, J. S., *Beyond the Information Given: Studies in the Psychology of Knowing*, ed. Jeremy Anglin. New York: Norton, 1973.

CEMREL Newsletter, Spring, 1973, 10646 St. Charles Rock Road, St. Ann, Missouri 63074.

Chittenden, E. A. et al. Analysis of an approach to open education, Interim Report. Princeton, 1970.

DeBoer, John J. and Dollman, Martha, *The Teaching of Reading.* New York: Holt, Rinehart, Winston, 1970.

Dewey, John, *Interest and Effort in Education.* Boston: Houghton Mifflin, 1913.

Drachler, Norman, Education and Politics in Large Cities, 1950-1970. NSSE Yearbook, *The Politics of Education.* Chicago: University of Chicago Press, 1977.

Durkin, Dolores, *Teaching Them to Read.* Boston: Allyn and Bacon, 1970.

Elkind, David, Piaget and Montessori, *Harvard Educational Review, Vol. 37.* Cambridge, 1967.

ETS Developments, Volume XX, Number 2. Princeton: Educational Testing Service, 1973.

Flavell, John H., *The Developmental Psychology of Jean Piaget.* New York: Nordstrom Press, 1963.

Harris, Larry A. and Smith, Carl B., *Reading Instruction Through Diagnostic Teaching*. New York: Holt, Rinehart and Winston, 1972.

Hemphill, J. K., The Relationship between research and evaluation studies. N.S.S.E. Yearbook, *Educational Evaluation: New Roles, New Means*. Chicago: University of Chicago Press, 1969.

Hummel, R. and Nagle, J., *Urban Education in America*. New York: Oxford University Press, 1973.

Isaacs, N., The Wider Significance of Piaget's Work and Piaget and Progressive Education, *Some Aspects of Piaget's Work*. New York: National Frobel Foundation, 1955.

Kaplan, S., Kaplan, J., Madsen, S., and Taylor, B., *Change for Children*. Pacific Palisades, California: Goodyear Publishing Co., 1973.

Kibler, R. J., Barker, L. L., and Miles, D. T., *Behavioral Objectives and Instruction*. Boston: Allyn and Bacon, Inc., 1970.

Lovell, K., *The Growth of Basic Mathematical and Science Concepts in Children*. London: University of London Press, 1962.

Mager, R. F., *Preparing Instructional Objectives*. Belmont, California: Fearon Publishers, 1962.

Maier, Henry W., *Three Theories of Child Development*. New York: Harper and Row, Revised Edition, 1969.

Montessori, Maria, *The Montessori Method*. Cambridge, Massachusetts: Robert Bentley, Inc., 1964.

Morgan, Lorraine L., A Model for Preservice Education of Elementary Reading Teachers, in *Reading Methods and Teacher Improvement*, N. B. Smith, Ed., International Reading Association, 1971.

_____., and Taylor, Ann Baldwin. Pre- and Inservice Preparation for Teachers of Young Children. Paper presented at Keystone State Reading Association, Philadelphia, Pa., 1972.

_____., Richman, Vivien C. and Taylor, Ann Baldwin, Evaluation Report of the British Educators' Visit. Mimeographed paper, Chatham College, Pittsburgh, Pa., 1973.

Norwich-Pittsburgh, Mimeographed Report, Norwich Teachers' Centre, M. E. Ellson, Coordinator. Norwich, England: 1973.

Pi Lamda Theta, *Educational Horizons*, Vol. 51, No. 2, King-Stoops, Joyce. Winter 1972-73, Profiled Instruction, page 86-89.

Piaget, Jean, *Play, Dreams and Imitation in Childhood*. New York: Norton, 1962.

_____., *The Psychology of Intelligence*. London: Routledge & Kegan Paul, Ltd., 1950.

_____., *Six Psychological Studies*. New York: Random House, 1967.

_____., *The Construction of Reality and the Child*. New York: Basic Books, Inc., 1954.

Plowman, P. D., *Behavioral Objectives*, Chicago: Science Research Associates, 1971.

Rance, P., *Record Keeping in the Progressive Primary School*. London: Ward Lock Educational Co., 1972.

Research and Information Services for Education (RISE), Vol. 4, no. 8, June, 1973, 198 Allendale Road, King of Prussia, Pa. 19406.

Ridgeway, L. and Lawton, I., *Family Grouping in the Primary School*. New York: Agathon Press, Inc., 1968.

Shane, Harold G., Prospectus and prerequisites for the improvement of elementary education: 1973-1985, N.S.S.E. Yearbook. Chicago: University of Chicago Press, 1973.

Silberman, Charles, *Crisis in the Classroom*. New York: Random House, 1970.

Silvaroli, Nicholas, *Classroom Reading Inventory*. Dubuque, Iowa: Wm. C. Brown and Company, 1973.

Tanner, J. and Inhelder, B. (Eds.), *Discussions on Child Development*. Vol. 1, London: Tavistock, 1956.

Taylor, Ann Baldwin. A Study of Open Classroom Environments in Early Childhood Education and Implications for Teacher Education. Unpublished doctoral dissertation, University of Pittsburgh, Pittsburgh, Pa., 1972.

Taylor, Joy, *Organizing and Integrating the Infant Day*. London: George Allen and Unwin Ltd., 1971.

Vargas, J. S., *Writing Worthwhile Behavioral Objectives*. New York: Harper and Row, 1972.

Weinstein, G., Fantini, M., *Toward Humanistic Education*. New York: Praeger Publishers, Inc., 1970.

NEW DIRECTIONS IN ETHNIC STUDIES: MINORITIES IN AMERICA by David
    Claerbaut, Editor Perfect Bound   LC# 80-69327
    ISBN 0-86548-025-7 $9.95
COLLECTING, CULTURING, AND CARING FOR LIVING MATERIALS: GUIDE FOR
    TEACHER, STUDENT AND HOBBYIST by William E. Claflin   Perfect
    Bound   LC# 80-69329   ISBN 0-86548-026-5 $8.50
TEACHING ABOUT THE OTHER AMERICANS: MINORITIES IN UNITED STATES
    HISTORY by Ann Curry Perfect Bound   LC# 80-69120
    ISBN 0-86548-028-1 $8.95
MULTICULTURAL TRANSACTIONS: A WORKBOOK FOCUSING ON COMMUNICATION
    BETWEEN GROUPS by James S. DeLo and William A. Green   Perfect
    Bound   LC# 80-69328   ISBN 0-86548-030-3 $11.50
LEARNING TO TEACH by Richard B. Dierenfield   Perfect Bound
    LC# 80-69119   ISBN 0-86548-031-1 $10.95
LEARNING TO THINK--TO LEARN by M. Ann Dirkes   Perfect Bound
    LC# 80-65613   ISBN 0-86548-032-X $11.50
PLAY IN PRESCHOOL MAINSTREAMED AND HANDICAPPED SETTINGS by Anne Cairns
    Federlein   Perfect Bound   LC# 80-65612   ISBN 0-86548-035-4
    $10.50
THE NATURE OF LEADERSHIP FOR HISPANICS AND OTHER MINORITIES by
    Ernest Yutze Flores   Perfect Bound   LC# 80-69239
    ISBN 0-86548-036-2 $10.95
THE MINI-GUIDE TO LEADERSHIP by Ernest Yutze Flores   Perfect Bound
    LC# 80-83627   ISBN 0-86548-037-0 $5.50
THOUGHTS, TROUBLES AND THINGS ABOUT READING FROM THE CRADLE THROUGH
    GRADE THREE by Carolyn T. Gracenin   Perfect Bound
    LC# 80-65611   ISBN 0-86548-038-9 $14.95
BETWEEN TWO CULTURES: THE VIETNAMESE IN AMERICA by Alan B. Henkin and
    Liem Thanh Nguyen   Perfect Bound   LC# 80-69333
    ISBN 0-86548-039-7 $7.95
PERSONALITY CHARACTERISTICS AND DISCIPLINARY ATTITUDES OF CHILD-
    ABUSING MOTHERS by Alan L. Evans   Perfect Bound   LC# 80-69240
    ISBN 0-86548-033-8 $11.95
PARENTAL EXPECTATIONS AND ATTITUDES ABOUT CHILDREARING IN HIGH RISK
    VS. LOW RISK CHILD ABUSING FAMILIES by Gary C. Rosenblatt
    Perfect Bound   LC# 79-93294   ISBN 0-86548-020-6 $10.00
CHILD ABUSE AS VIEWED BY SUBURBAN ELEMENTARY SCHOOL TEACHERS by David
    A. Pelcovitz   Perfect Bound   LC# 79-93295   ISBN 0-86548-019-2
    $10.00
PHYSICAL CHILD ABUSE: AN EXPANDED ANALYSIS by James R. Seaberg
    Perfect Bound   LC# 79-93293   ISBN 0-86548-021-4 $10.00
THE DISPOSITION OF REPORTED CHILD ABUSE by Marc F. Maden   Perfect
    Bound   LC# 79-93296   ISBN 0-86548-016-8 $10.00
EDUCATIONAL AND PSYCHOLOGICAL PROBLEMS OF ABUSED CHILDREN by James
    Christiansen   Perfect Bound   LC# 79-93303   ISBN 0-86548-003-6
    $10.00
DEPENDENCY, FRUSTRATION TOLERANCE, AND IMPULSE CONTROL IN CHILD ABUSERS
    by Don Kertzman   Perfect Bound   LC# 79-93297   ISBN 86548-015-X
    $10.00
SUCCESSFUL STUDENT TEACHING: A HANDBOOK FOR ELEMENTARY AND SECONDARY
    STUDENT TEACHERS by Fillmer Hevener, Jr.   Perfect Bound
    LC# 80-69332   ISBN 0-86548-040-0 $8.95
BLACK COMMUNICATION IN WHITE SOCIETY by Roy Cogdell and Sybil Wilson
    Perfect Bound   LC# 79-93302   ISBN 0-86548-004-4 $13.00

SCHOOL VANDALISM: CAUSE AND CURE by Robert Bruce Williams and Joseph
     L. Venturini   Perfect Bound   LC# 80-69230   ISBN 0-86548-060-5
     $9.50
LEADERS, LEADING, AND LEADERSHIP by Harold W. Boles   Perfect Bound
     LC# 80-65616   ISBN 0-86548-023-0 $14.95
LEGAL OUTLOOK: A MESSAGE TO COLLEGE AND UNIVERSITY PEOPLE by Ulysses
     V. Spiva   Perfect Bound   LC# 80-69232   ISBN 0-86548-057-5
     $9.95
THE NAKED CHILD THE LONG RANGE EFFECTS OF FAMILY AND SOCIAL NUDITY
     by Dennis Craig Smith   Perfect Bound   LC# 80-69234
     ISBN 0-86548-056-7 $7.95
SIGNIFICANT INFLUENCE PEOPLE: A SIP OF DISCIPLINE AND ENCOURAGEMENT
     by Joseph C. Rotter, Johnnie McFadden and Gary D. Kannenberg
     Perfect Bound   LC# 80-69233   ISBN 0-86548-055-9 $8.95
LET'S HAVE FUN WITH ENGLISH by Ruth Rackmill   Perfect Bound
     LC# 80-68407   ISBN 0-86548-061-3 $6.95
CHILDREN'S PERCEPTIONS OF ELDERLY PERSONS by Lillian A. Phenice
     Perfect Bound   LC# 80-65604   ISBN 0-86548-054-0 $10.50
URBAN EDUCATION: AN ANNOTATED BIBLIOGRAPHY by Arnold G. Parks
     Perfect Bound   LC# 80-69234   ISBN 0-86548-053-2 $9.50
DYNAMICS OF CLASSROOM STRUCTURE by Charles J. Nier   Perfect Bound
     LC# 80-69330   ISBN 0-86548-052-4 $11.50
SOCIOLOGY IN BONDAGE: AN INTRODUCTION TO GRADUATE STUDY by Harold A.
     Nelson   Perfect Bound   LC# 80-65605   ISBN 0-86548-051-6 $9.95
BEYOND THE OPEN CLASSROOM: TOWARD INFORMAL EDUCATION by Lorraine L.
     Morgan, Vivien C. Richman and Ann Baldwin Taylor   Perfect Bound
     LC# 80-69235   ISBN 0-86548-050-8 $9.50
INTRODUCTORY SOCIOLOGY: LECTURES, READINGS AND EXERCISES by Gordon D.
     Morgan   Perfect Bound   LC# 80-65606   ISBN 0-86548-049-4
     $10.50
THE STUDENT TEACHER ON THE FIRING LINE by D. Eugene Meyer   Perfect
     Bound   LC# 80-69236   ISBN 0-86548-048-6 $11.95
VALUES ORIENTATION IN SCHOOL by Johnnie McFadden and Joseph C. Rotter
     Perfect Bound   LC# 80-69238   ISBN 0-86548-045-1 $4.50
MOVEMENT THEMES: TOPICS FOR EARLY CHILDHOOD LEARNING THROUGH CREATIVE
     MOVEMENT by Barbara Stewart Jones   Perfect Bound   LC# 80-65608
     ISBN 0-86548-042-7 $8.50
FROM BIRTH TO TWELVE: HOW TO BE A SUCCESSFUL PARENT TO INFANTS AND
     CHILDREN by Gary D. Kannenberg   Perfect Bound   LC# 80-69331
     ISBN 0-86548-043-5 $7.95